Alabama Bucket List Adventure Guide

Explore Over 100 Must-See Wonders!

Angela Hall

Bridge Press

support@bridgepress.org

Please consider writing a review!

Just visit: purplelink.org/review

ISBN: 978-1-955149-42-6

FREE BONUS

Find Out 31 Incredible Places You Can
Visit Next! Just Go To:

purplelink.org/travel

Table of Contents

Haleyville

Hoover

Houston

Huntsville

Leed

How to Use This Book

Welcome to your very own adventure guide to exploring the many wonders of Alabama. Not only does this book lay out the most wonderful places to visit and sights to see in the vast state, but it provides driving directions and GPS coordinates for Google Maps to make exploring that much easier.

Adventure Guide

Sorted by region, this guide offers over 100 amazing wonders found in Alabama for you to go see and explore. These can be visited in any order, and this book will help keep track of where you've been and where to look forward to going next. Each portion describes the area or place, what to look for, how to get there, and what you may need to bring along.

GPS Coordinates

As you can imagine, not all of the locations in this book have a physical address. Fortunately, some of our listed wonders are either located within a national park or reserve or are near a city, town, or place of business. For those that are not associated with a specific location, it is easiest to map it using GPS coordinates.

Luckily, Google has a system of codes that converts the coordinates into pin-drop locations that Google Maps can interpret and navigate.

Each adventure in this guide will include the GPS coordinates along with general directions on how to find the location.

You must be prepared for poor cell signals. It is recommended that you route your location and ensure that the directions are accessible offline. Depending on your device and the distance of some locations, you may need to travel with a backup battery source.

About Alabama

Alabama, also known as the "Yellowhammer State,"
"Cotton State," and "Heart of Dixie," is a beautiful state
that attracts residents and travelers from all over the
country. Alabama joined the United States on December 4,
1819, after previously being a Spanish territory. With its
diverse geography, visitors are drawn to this area to
experience nature and college football. Alabama is the 13th
largest state in the U.S., and the most popular cities to live
in are Birmingham, Montgomery, and Huntsville.

Landscape and Climate

The landscape of Alabama is diverse and includes a wide
variety of terrains, from mountains to breathtaking beaches.
There are a plethora of valleys, flatlands, lakes, caves, and
swamps as you come down off of the Appalachian
Mountains. Mountains and hills from the Tennessee Valley
are located along the northern part of the state.

Alabama is home to a number of unique butterfly species
that can be found all over the state. The warm climate
makes it possible for these butterflies to live, especially
with the presence of the Tennessee River, which runs
through a good portion of the state. All of its rivers and

lakes drain into the Gulf of Mexico, located at the state's southern border.

The climate in Alabama is very average, but the temperature has been known to rise and fall based on the winds coming off of the Gulf of Mexico. The average yearly temperature is 64 degrees Fahrenheit, and rain with severe storms is a common occurrence.

Plant and Animal Life

Due to the warm temperatures year-round in Alabama, there are over one hundred different types of trees in the area. The majority of these are located in the northern part of the state, in the Tennessee Valley Mountains.

With the number of trees present, birds are abundant as well. From cardinals to mockingbirds, owls and eagles, there are birds everywhere to observe. While it might seem like more of a western creature, armadillos have made their way into the state and now call Alabama home.

Snakes are present in most of the bodies of water found around the state, including poisonous rattlesnakes, copperheads, and water moccasins. Always be on the alert when exploring swamps, as alligators are present, especially when you travel closer to the coast.

People and Resources

The biggest draw to the state of Alabama is the iron and steel industry, which originated in Birmingham. Deposits of limestone, coal and iron make this state rich in minerals. White marble is also present, which is used most commonly as pigment for paper.

Natural gas is notable along the coast, as well as petroleum by the use of wells. Coal-fired thermal plants power the majority of Alabama's electricity. All of these industries create a need for jobs, which is another reason why so many people make Alabama their home.

Lake Martin

Lake Martin is one of the largest manmade lakes in the entire country, making it a great destination for swimming, water skiing, fishing, boating, golfing, or camping. The lake has numerous fishing tournaments, jazz festivals, and fireworks shows. Tourists usually enjoy visiting Lake Martin to viewing the eagle's nest, hanging out at the beaches, eating at the restaurants, and camping. While there are a lot of areas where swimming might look appealing, always be careful because people have spotted alligators in the water, and there are no lifeguards on duty.

Best Time to Visit: Any time of year

Pass/Permit/Fees: Free

Closest City or Town: Alexander City, AL

How to Get There: From Alexander City, head west toward Court Square, turn right onto Court Square, turn right at the first cross street onto Main St., continue onto Church St., turn left to stay on Church St., then turn right onto Madison St. Continue onto AL-63 S/Cherokee Rd. (pass Caldwell Electronics), turn left onto Tecumseh Point Rd., turn left onto Blount Point Rd. Continue straight onto Russell Point Rd., turn right to stay on Russell Point Rd. and you will arrive at your destination.

GPS Coordinates: 32.73717° N, -85.94297° W

Did You Know? Lake Martin is the largest manmade lake in Alabama, with over 880 miles of shoreline. When it was first created, it was the largest manmade lake in the *world*.

Mobile Bay

Mobile Bay is a small area where the Gulf of Mexico juts into the shoreline of Alabama. The area is also an estuary because the Tensaw and Mobile Rivers meet the ocean at this point.

The bay is 31 miles long by 24 miles wide and can be up to 75 feet deep. About once a year, the shrimp and fish are washed up to the surface of the water, and residents of the area refer to this time of year as "Jubilee." As with any town or area along the coast, there is a high chance of hurricanes throughout the year, so always be aware and prepared in the event of a bad storm rolling through.

Best Time to Visit: March-May and September-November

Pass/Permit/Fees: Free

Closest City or Town: Allenville, AL

How to Get There: From Allenville, head north on St. Stephens Rd. toward White Ave., turn right onto St. Charles Ave., turn right onto Dr. Martin Luther King Jr. Ave., turn left onto Beauregard St., turn right onto N. Water St., and you will arrive in Mobile Bay.

GPS Coordinates: 30.46989° N, -87.99627° W

Did You Know? Mobile Bay was originally used by Spanish explorers in the 1500s who named the area "Bay of the Holy Spirit."

Conecuh National Forest

The Conecuh National Forest in Alabama is an 83,000-acre forest that covers portions of both Alabama and Florida. At the national forest are hiking trails that extend 20 miles along the coast of the state.

"Conecuh" originally means "land of cane," which is fitting considering the trail runs along canebrakes. Here you can find swamps, pitcher plant bogs, and pine forests.

As with the other national forests in Alabama, the headquarters can be found in Montgomery, AL.

Best Time to Visit: November-March when the weather is cooler

Pass/Permit/Fees: Must obtain a pass, but they are free

Closest City or Town: Andalusia, AL

How to Get There: From Andalusia, head south toward Court Square, turn left onto Troy St. Turn right onto Court Square, continue onto S. 3 Notch St., turn left onto US-29 S/Western Bypass and follow US-29 S, turn left onto Dixie Hwy. and you will arrive at your destination.

GPS Coordinates: 31.07820° N, -86.61548° W

Did You Know? The Conecuh National Forest is the southern-most forest in Alabama and stretches across the Alabama/Florida state line.

Cheaha State Park

The Cheaha State Park is found in the middle of the Talladega National Forest, at 2,407 feet above sea level. The Creek Indians of the area nicknamed this park "Chaha," which means high place. Fishing, camping, lodging, and exploration are all popular activities in this area. The state park offers beauty to be discovered in the foothills of the Appalachian Mountains. The park extends 2,799 acres and has the highest summit in all of Alabama.

Best Time to Visit: Any time of year

Pass/Permit/Fees: Age 0-3: Free, Age 4-11: $2, Age 12+: $5, Parks for patriots, veterans, and active military: Free (ID required). A day pass includes admission to Mountain Park, Vista Cliffside Restaurant and Overlook, and Lake Recreation Area.

Closest City or Town: Anniston, Oxford, and Talladega, AL

How to Get There: The park recommends that travelers use Talladega Scenic Dr., also known as Alabama Hwy. 281. Another option is to use Hwy. 49, which connects with Hwy. 281. The most scenic option is to take Cheaha Rd. (County Rd. 42), from Munford, AL. This road is windy and not recommended for large recreational vehicles.

GPS Coordinates: 33.47013° N, -85.81336° W

Did You Know? The entire state park is named after Mount Cheaha, a quartzite rock mountain.

Chewacla State Park

The Chewacla State Park is made up of 696 acres of land to explore. With a lake, swimming area, playground, picnic area, cabins, and trails for hiking or biking, the park has a lot to offer visitors.

Lake Chewacla is available for fishing, but if you do not catch any bream, bass, crappie, or catfish, you are also welcome to try fishing in the two creeks located on the state park premises. Canoes and kayaks are allowed, but boats with motors are prohibited.

Best Time to Visit: Any time of year

Pass/Permit/Fees: $4 per person

Closest City or Town: Auburn, AL

How to Get There: From Auburn, head south toward E. Glenn Ave., turn left toward E. Glenn Ave., turn left onto E. Glenn Ave., turn right onto N. Gay St., turn right onto E. University Dr., take a slight left onto Wrights Mill Rd., turn left onto Murphy Dr., and you will reach your destination. Chewacla State Park, 124 Shell Toomer Pkwy., Auburn, AL 36830

GPS Coordinates: 32.55414° N, -85.47783° W

Did You Know? The lake at the Chewacla State Park stretches for 26 acres and can be used for swimming. There are no lifeguards on duty, so swim at your own risk.

Robert Trent Jones Golf Trail

The Robert Trent Jones Golf Trail is made for golf fanatics who enjoy spending time on the green. The trail consists of 468 holes, all championship caliber. This golf trail is the largest golf course ever created. It consists of 26 different golf courses in 11 different locations across Alabama.

Best Time to Visit: Any time of year

Pass/Permit/Fees: Championship 18 Hole Green Fees: $65+ tax, Championship 9 Hole Green Fees: 60% of rack rate, Short Course Green Fees: $18 for 18 holes, Junior Rates (17 and under): $27 for 18 holes. Carts are also available for rent as well, the price paid per person per round.

Closest City or Town: The trail sites are: Cambian Ridge in Greenville, AL; Capitol Hill in Prattville, AL; Grand National in Auburn/Opelika, AL; Hampton Cove in Huntsville, AL; Highland Oakes in Dothan, AL; Lakewood Club in Point Clear, AL; Magnolia Grove in Mobile, AL; Oxmoor Valley in Birmingham, AL; Ross Bridge in Hoover, AL; Silver Lakes in Anniston/Gadsden, AL, and The Shoals in Muscle Shoals, AL.

How to Get There: There is at least one golf trail in every major city listed above.

GPS Coordinates: All over the state

Did You Know? The RTJ Golf Trail was built in 1992 to help with the Retirement Systems of Alabama.

Birmingham Civil Rights Institute

The Birmingham Civil Rights Institute exists to "enlighten each generation about civil and human rights by exploring our common past and working together in the present to build a better future," according to their mission statement.

At the Birmingham Civil Rights Institute, guests will hear the story of the history of Birmingham and understand the importance of the Civil Rights Movement.

Best Time to Visit: Any time of year, closed Sunday-Monday, open Tuesday-Saturday 10 a.m.-3 p.m.

Pass/Permit/Fees: Adult: $15, Senior/College Student/Youth (4-12th grade): $13, Children under 3rd grade: Free

Closest City or Town: Birmingham, AL

How to Get There:
From Birmingham, head southwest on 6th Ave. N toward 18th St. N, turn left at the third cross street onto 16th St. N, and your destination will be on the right. 520 16th St. N, Birmingham, AL 35203

GPS Coordinates: 33.51752° N, -86.80962° W

Did You Know?
The Birmingham Civil Rights Institute was built in November of 1992.

Birmingham Museum of Art

The Birmingham Museum of Art is a non-profit organization that relies on corporate partners and donors to help fund all programs and events. This museum showcases more than 24,000 paintings, drawings, art pieces, and sculptures representing many different cultures in the Southeast.

Located in the heart of the city, the Birmingham Museum of Art has 3.9 acres of artifacts to explore and observe. One of the most viewed collections here is the Kress Collection of Renaissance and Baroque paintings from the late 13th century to c.1750.

Best Time to Visit: Tuesday-Saturday 10 a.m.-5 p.m., Sunday Noon-5 p.m.

Pass/Permit/Fees: Free

Closest City or Town: Birmingham, AL

How to Get There: From Birmingham, head northwest on 19th St. N toward 6th Ave. N Alley/Park Pl., turn right onto Reverend Abraham Woods Jr. Blvd., turn right onto Richard Arrington Jr. Blvd. N, turn left, and your destination will be on the right. 2000 Reverend Abraham Woods Jr. Blvd., Birmingham, AL 35203

GPS Coordinates: 33.52394° N, -86.80938° W

Did You Know? The Birmingham Museum of Art originally opened in 1885 and showcased over 40 galleries.

Birmingham Zoo

A great activity for the entire family is to visit the Birmingham Zoo. Here, your family can enjoy a number of different plants, a few hands-on activities, and observe more than 950 different animals!

Throughout the year, several different events and activities are held to help draw guests to the zoo to educate and enrich the lives of children and adults. The Birmingham Zoo is noted as one of the state's most popular attractions, so you must see all of the animals here during your visit!

Best Time to Visit: Any time of year

Pass/Permit/Fees: Adult: $17.95, Children (ages 2-12): $12.95, Seniors (65+): $14.95, Infant: Free

Closest City or Town: Birmingham, AL

How to Get There: From Birmingham, head southeast on 19th St. N toward 5th Ave. N Alley (pass by Wells Fargo on the left). Turn left onto 3rd Ave. N, take the ramp onto US-280 E/US-31 S, merge onto the highway, take the exit toward 21st Ave. Turn left onto 21st Ave. S, turn right onto Cahaba Rd. at the traffic circle, take the first exit, take a slight left, turn left, and you will arrive at your destination. 2630 Cahaba Rd, Birmingham, AL 35223

GPS Coordinates: 33.48765° N, -86.77919° W

Did You Know? The Birmingham Zoo opened in 1955!

Cahaba Blueway

The Cahaba River is one of the most beautiful rivers in the United States and runs right through the center of Alabama. This river serves as a source of drinking water for multiple counties and a recreational hotspot for many Alabama locals.

Paddling, floating, fishing, and swimming are a few of the reasons that people are drawn to the Cahaba Blueway. The Cahaba Blueway is a program by the University of Alabama Center for Economic Development to help make the river a place for anyone and everyone to enjoy and benefit from.

Best Time to Visit: Any time of year, but it is not safe to swim after it rains or when the water is muddy.

Pass/Permit/Fees: Free

Closest City or Town: Birmingham, AL

How to Get There: From Birmingham, head southeast on 19th St. N toward 5th Ave. N Alley (pass Wells Fargo Bank on the left), turn left onto 3rd Ave. N, take the ramp onto US-280 E/US-31 S. Take the University Blvd. exit, turn right onto 8th Ave. S/University Blvd., turn right onto 25th S. Turn right at the first cross street onto 7th Ave. S and your destination will be on the right. Cahaba River Society, 2717 Ave S #205, Birmingham, AL 35233

GPS Coordinates: 33.51099° N, -86.78886° W

Did You Know? The Cahaba River flows for 191 miles and connects very different economic regions of the state.

Don Kresge Memorial Museum

The Don Kresge Memorial Museum is located in the middle of Birmingham and allows guests to explore vintage radios. Even if you are not interested in the music of the past, it allows you to see the technology transformation throughout history.

The museum offers reading rooms that allow you to learn more about the legacy of the radio, in addition to numerous artifacts from the past. The Don Kresge Memorial Museum also includes information on the evolution from radio to television.

Best Time to Visit: Any time of year, open M-F from 9 a.m.-5 p.m.

Pass/Permit/Fees: Unknown

Closest City or Town: Birmingham, AL

How to Get There: From Birmingham, head southwest on 6th Ave. N toward 18th St. N, and your destination will be on the right. 600 18th St. N, Birmingham, AL 35203

GPS Coordinates: 33.52111° N, -86.81185° W

Did You Know? At the Don Kresge Memorial Museum, guests can observe and listen to radios that were made over 50 years ago!

Legion Field

Legion Field is located in Birmingham, Alabama. It is used as a football stadium and hosting other large outdoor events. The seating capacity at this field is 71,594, and it is nicknamed the "Football Capital of the South."

The stadium is commonly referred to as "The Old Gray Lady" and is the location for UAB Blazers football, Birmingham Bowl, local high school games, musical festivals, and other sporting events.

Best Time to Visit: Any time of year

Pass/Permit/Fees: Average cost to attend an event is $50.60, but ticket prices depend on the event being held and the seats selected.

Closest City or Town: Birmingham, AL

How to Get There: From Birmingham, head southwest on 6th Ave. N toward 18th St. N, turn left onto 6th St. N, turn right onto Graymont Ave. N. Turn right, and you will reach your destination. 400 Graymont Ave. W, Birmingham, AL 35204

GPS Coordinates: 33.51206° N, -86.84298° W

Did You Know? This historical football stadium is famous for hosting the BBVA Compass Bowl as well as home games for the university Blazer team.

McWane Science Center

The McWane Science Center is found in downtown Birmingham. The facility is home to an aquarium and an IMAX Dome Theater, in addition to science exhibits. This building was previously the Loveman's department store but was opened to the public in 1998.

The bottom level of the science center has more than 50 different freshwater species, including sharks and stingrays. One of the most popular exhibits is the shark tooth under a microscope exhibit that shows how water pollution affects the animals in the water.

The upper level has a small children's museum as well as the Alabama Collections Center, featuring more than 500,000 items from the Red Mountain Museum.

Best Time to Visit: Any time of year

Pass/Permit/Fees: Tickets cost anywhere from $8-$16

Closest City or Town: Birmingham, AL

How to Get There: From Birmingham, head southeast on 19th St N. toward 5th Ave. N Alley (pass by Wells Fargo on the left), turn right onto 2nd Ave. N and your destination will be on the right. 200 19th St. N, Birmingham, AL 35203

GPS Coordinates: 33.51544° N, -86.80685° W

Did You Know? The entire McWane Science Center is four stories high!

Red Mountain Park

Red Mountain Park is a public park with an urban feel that marks the exact location where the city of Birmingham originated. Within the park, there are closed mines as well as other markers of the history of the city.

This park has 1,500 acres of land, which includes 15 miles of trails, three treehouses for your exploration, the largest dog park in the state (known as Remy's Dog Park), a zipline, as well as an adventure tower.

Best Time to Visit: Any time of year, but the summer months will be warm.

Pass/Permit/Fees: Free, but donations are welcome and appreciated.

Closest City or Town: Birmingham, AL

How to Get There: From Birmingham, head southwest on 6th Ave. N toward 18th St, turn left onto 10th St. N. Merge onto I-65 S via the ramp to Montgomery. Merge to I-65 S, Exit 258 for Green Springs Ave. Keep right at the fork and merge onto Green Springs Ave., continue onto Dennison Ave. SW, turn left onto Martin Luther King Jr Dr, continue to Montevallo Rd SW, turn right onto Industrial Ln, turn right onto Lyon Ln, turn right at Frankfurt Dr, and you will reach your destination. 2011 Frankfurt Dr. Birmingham, AL 35211

GPS Coordinates: 33.44556° N, -86.86203° W

Did You Know? Red Mountain Park is two times the size of Central Park in NYC!

Ruffner Mountain Nature Center

The Ruffner Mountain Nature Center is found in Birmingham and consists of 227 acres of forest land. This area provides an opportunity to educate the public on environmental subjects and has numerous trails for hiking and observing wildlife. The hiking trails are available for the public any time of the day, from sunup to sundown. If you are traveling through the Alabama Birding Trail, you will be making a stop at the Ruffner Mountain Nature Center along the way.

Best Time to Visit: Any time of year, closed on Mondays

Pass/Permit/Fees: $3 hiking trail fee

Closest City or Town: Birmingham, AL

How to Get There: From Birmingham, head northwest on 19th St. N toward 6th Ave. N Alley/Park Pl. Turn right onto Reverend Abraham Woods Jr Blvd., and turn left onto 25th St. N. Take the ramp onto I-20E/I-59 N, merge onto I-20 E/I-59 N. Keep left at the fork to continue on I-59 N, follow the signs for I-59 N/Gadsden, take Exit 132 for US-11 N/1st Ave. Merge onto US-11 N/1st Ave. N. Turn right onto 83rd St. N, continue onto Rugby Ave, turn left onto 81st St S, turn left at 81st Alley S. Turn right to reach 1214 81st St. S, Birmingham, AL 35206

GPS Coordinates: 33.55888° N, -86.70668° W

Did You Know? This nature preserve is 1,040 acres and is privately owned, with 11 miles of nature trails that allow you to bring your pets.

Vulcan Park and Museum

The Vulcan Park and Museum is home to the largest cast-iron statue found in the entire world. The statue found here is a locally recognized symbol for the city of Birmingham, showing the origins of the city forged of iron and steel.

Located on 10 acres of urban green space, visitors can admire and observe the statue as well as visit the interactive museum. Guests can broaden their historical knowledge of Birmingham when exploring this area.

Best Time to Visit: Any time of year

Pass/Permit/Fees: Adult (ages 13+): $6, Seniors/Military: $5, Children (ages 5-12): $4, children under 4: Free

Closest City or Town: Birmingham, AL

How to Get There: From Birmingham, head southeast on 19th St. N toward 5th Ave. N Alley (pass by the Wells Fargo Bank on the left), turn left onto 3rd Ave. N. Take the ramp on the left to US-280 E/US-31 S, merge onto US-280 E/US-31 S, take the exit toward 21st Ave. Turn right onto 21st Ave. S, continue straight onto Valley Ave., turn right onto Valley View Dr. Turn left to stay on Valley View Dr., turn right, and you will arrive at your destination. 1701 Valley View Dr., Birmingham, AL 35209

GPS Coordinates: 33.49167° N, -86.79522° W

Did You Know? You can climb to the observation balcony on the Vulcan statue and get the best views of the city, 124 feet above the ground.

Russell Cave National Monument

The Russell Cave National Monument can be found in the northeastern part of the state, near Bridgeport, Alabama. Native Americans used the large entrance into the cave as a means of protection, especially in the winter months. With a guided tour of the area, you can expect to learn so much more about this interesting area and the people once living there. The cave itself stretches for 7.2 miles and is known as the third-longest cave in the country. This is another destination located on the Alabama Birding Trail.

Best Time to Visit: Any time during the day

Pass/Permit/Fees: Free

Closest City or Town: Bridgeport, AL

How to Get There: From Bridgeport, head north on Johnson St. toward Alabama Ave., turn left at the first cross street onto Alabama Ave. Turn right onto 7th St. Turn left at the first cross street onto Broadway Ave., take a slight right onto Co. Rd. 75/Lewis Payne Dr. (continue to follow CR 75), turn right onto Co Rd. 98. Turn le, and the monument will be right there. Russell Cave National Monument, 3729 County Rd., 98 Bridgeport, AL 35740

GPS Coordinates: 34.97665° N, -85.81422° W

Did You Know? There is a natural spring that runs inside the cave and continues to travel beneath the surface of the ground for 1.5 miles. This river eventually turns into the Tennessee River.

Stone Cuts Trail

Stone Cuts Trail is a 2.4-mile loop for hiking or biking. This trail starts and ends in the same location, with views of Alabama wildflowers, and it is open year-round.

Many people who have previously taken this trail have noted that it is very well kept, hilly in areas, but overall rated as a moderate skill-level trail. With rock formations along the way, the Stone Cuts Trail is interesting and enjoyable for outdoor adventurers.

Best Time to Visit: Any time of year

Pass/Permit/Fees: $5 per adult, $2 per child/senior

Closest City or Town: Brownsboro, AL

How to Get There: From Brownsboro, head southwest on Brownsboro Rd. toward Stone Dr. Turn right onto US-72 W, turn left onto Dug Hill Rd., take a slight right. Take another slight right onto US-431/Governors Dr. SE, take a slight right onto Monte Sano Blvd SE. Turn right onto Nolen Ave. SE and a slight left onto Bankhead Pkwy. NE.

GPS Coordinates: 34.75026° N, -86.50431° W

Did You Know? Along the Stone Cuts Trail are numerous limestone formations that make this trail popular and well-known.

Orange Beach

Orange Beach is one of the most relaxing beaches Alabama has to offer, next to Gulf Shores. At Orange Beach, you will find golf courses, hiking and biking trails, areas for kayaking or canoeing, as well as numerous opportunities to fish.

The white sand found on Orange Beach is beautiful against the turquoise waters that crash onto the shores. Orange Beach has something to offer everyone, making it a great location for a family vacation.

Best Time to Visit: Early June (after Memorial Day), before or after July 4th, any time in August

Pass/Permit/Fees: Free

Closest City or Town: Caswell, AL

How to Get There: From Caswell, head northwest on Burkart Dr. toward Burkard Ln., turn left onto Alabama's Coastal Connection/Canal Rd. Turn left onto AL-161 S/Alabama's Coastal Connection/Orange Beach Blvd., turn right onto Alabama's Coastal Connection/Perdido Beach Blvd. and you will arrive at your destination.

GPS Coordinates: 30.28002° N, -87.57583° W

Did You Know? The beach was given the name "Orange Beach" after locals tried to grow oranges and grapefruit trees on the shoreline, only to not be successful!

DeSoto Caverns

In the foothills of the Appalachian Mountains is where the DeSoto Caverns are found, also known as "Alabama's Big Cave." Previously, this cave was used as a mine during the Civil War, and there is some proof of Native American use as well. Not only are there spectacular caves to discover, but here you can also dig for gemstones, explore the Lost Trail Maze, and ride amusement park rides. During the holiday seasons, there are lights and water shows that are breathtaking and very entertaining.

Best Time to Visit: Any time of year. During the summer months, it will be very cool, and during the winter months, it will be warm. It is open Monday-Thursday.

Pass/Permit/Fees: Rates are for all-inclusive tickets. Adult: $49.99, Child & Senior: $44.99

Closest City or Town: Childersburg, AL

How to Get There: From Childersburg, head north on 8th Ave. SW toward 1st St. SW, turn right onto 1st St SW, continue onto AL-26/ Desoto Caverns Pkwy. Turn left, in 85 ft. turn left again, and you will arrive at the Desoto Caverns. 5181 Desoto Caverns Pkwy., Childersburg, AL 35044

GPS Coordinates: 33.30700° N, -86.27746° W

Did You Know? Bones have been discovered here that date back to over 2,000 years ago! The DeSoto Caverns are often considered the most historic caverns in the country.

Livingston Lake

As one of the largest lakes in Alabama, Livingston Lake is a must-see place for travelers, especially those who enjoy fishing. On this lake, the types of fish you might catch range from catfish to bass. To access the water, there are three boat ramps. A fishing pier and two fish cleaning stations are available.

Swimming and boating are popular activities for this area but always proceed with caution when entering the water. Canoes and kayaks are available for rent on the weekends from 8:30 a.m.-3:30 p.m. Always be aware of your surroundings, as there are alligators in this lake!

Best Time to Visit: October, April, and March. July and August become very warm and make it uncomfortable for guests

Pass/Permit/Fees: $5 per day, per person ages 13+

Closest City or Town: Clanton, AL

How to Get There: From Clanton, head southwest on 1st Ave. toward 6th St. N, turn left at the first cross street onto 6th St. S. Turn left onto US-31 S/7th St. S (pass by Wendy's), turn left onto Co. Rd. 24, turn left onto Co. Rd. 59/Co. Rd. 706. Take a slight right onto Co. Rd. 542, turn right onto Co. Rd. 547, turn right onto Co. Rd. 710.

GPS Coordinates: 32.81568° N, -86.47167° W

Did You Know? While these waters are safe for swimming, there is evidence of alligators, and the fish caught are not necessarily safe for consumption.

Eastern Shore

It should come as no surprise that the Eastern Shore is found on the eastern part of the shoreline in Mobile, AL. This area of the state does not have strict boundaries, but it is thought to stretch from the north side of I-10 to Weeks Bay. The main thing that keeps this area thriving is the retail found around the Eastern Shore. Travelers come from near or far to visit the beach and stay in hotels or shop in this area. Golfing is available year-round as well as many nature trails. The Eastern Shore is full of Southern charm, seafood, and beautiful sunsets over the Mobile Bay.

Best Time to Visit: March-May and September-November

Pass/Permit/Fees: Free

Closest City or Town: Daphne, AL

How to Get There: From Daphne, head east on Belrose Ave. toward Eastern Shore Trail/Main St. Turn right onto Eastern Shore Trail/Main St., and you will arrive at the destination.

GPS Coordinates: 30.6693° N, -87.8492° W

Did You Know? In the Eastern Shore area, particularly Daphne, Alabama, there is a time of year where seafood such as blue crab, fish, and shrimp come to the surface of the water for anyone to grab for consumption. This time of year is referred to as "Jubilee," and the town of Daphne has often been called "The Jubilee City."

Alabama Birding Trail

Alabama's Birding Trail includes more than 280 places across the state to observe all of the beautiful birds. Popular birding trails include North Alabama Birding Trail, Alabama Coastal Birding Trail, Black Belt Birding Trail, Piedmont Plateau Birding Trail, West Alabama Birding Trail, Appalachian Highlands Birding Trail, and Wiregrass Birding Trail. If you enjoy birdwatching, then stopping by one of these trails will give you a lot of opportunities to spot Alabama's wildlife.

Best Time to Visit: Spring is the best time to visit, as the weather is comfortable, and everything is blooming. During the summer months, there are more birds present, but the humidity is also very high.

Pass/Permit/Fees: Free

Closest City or Town: The birding trails are located all over the entire state!

How to Get There: Depending on which Alabama Birding Trail you want to visit, there are various ways to get to each destination. Here is a website showing all of the different birding trails in the state.
https://alabamabirdingtrails.com/map/

GPS Coordinates: 34.69340° N, -87.08707 ° W (This is the GPS Coordinate for the West Alabama Birding Trail, one of the most popular trails to visit.)

Did You Know? Alabama has more than 430 bird species that have been documented and studied.

Carnegie Visual Arts Center

The Carnegie Visual Arts Center was first used as a library in 1904. Over time the building was updated and later opened in 2003 as Carnegie Visual Arts Center, where guests are welcome to explore and enjoy this educational venue.

The children's art program at this location is one of the most popular offerings, where children can enjoy many different hands-on activities. One of the most memorable exhibits is the Anne Frank Life in Words and Photos.

Best Time to Visit: Any time of year

Pass/Permit/Fees: Free, but donations are welcome

Closest City or Town: Decatur, AL

How to Get There: From Decatur, head southeast toward Lee St. NE, turn right onto Lee St NE. Turn right at the first cross street onto Ferry St. NE. Turn left onto Church St. NE, and your destination is on the left. 207 Church St. NE, Decatur, AL, 35601

GPS Coordinates: 34.61247° N, -86.98016° W

Did You Know? The Carnegie Visual Arts Center is one of the period original buildings and originally cost $8,500.

Cook Natural Science Museum

In Decatur, Alabama, is the Cook Natural Science Museum, a place where children and adults can spend the day doing hands-on science experiments and learning more about nature. The museum provides families with lasting memories from the activities and exhibits.

The museum also has several live animals, including fish, sea turtles, coral, jellyfish, snakes, alligators, and more. A store is at the museum for guests to purchase souvenirs, and there's an event venue for large gatherings and very elegant corporate dinners.

Best Time to Visit: Any time of the year

Pass/Permit/Fees: Adults (age 15+): $20, Seniors (65+)/Military: $17, Children under 2: Free

Closest City or Town: Decatur, AL

How to Get There: From Decatur, head southeast toward Lee St. NE, turn right onto Lee St. NE. Take a sharp left onto 2nd A.ve NE and turn left onto Moulton St. E. Turn left at the first cross street onto 4th Ave. NE and the destination will be on the left. 133 4th Ave. NE, Decatur AL, 35601

GPS Coordinates: 34.60529° N, -86.98274° W

Did You Know? The Cook Natural Science Museum has a restaurant in the facility called Nature's Table, where all healthy meals are served. From healthy wraps to protein bowls, you will leave full and feeling great from making a healthy choice with your food.

Delano Park

Nestled in the middle of the town of Decatur lies Delano Park, a beautiful area for guests to enjoy the outdoors. This park includes a large play area with four basketball goals, a bridge, volleyball nets, a badminton play area, a splash pad, a rose garden, a playground, and a one-mile walking trail.

Whether you are driving through the area or looking for a great place to stop for a picnic lunch, you can't go wrong by choosing Delano Park with the breathtaking rose garden. Splash pads are an excellent way for children to stay cool in the hot summer months, as well as experience a very safe way to play in the water.

Best Time to Visit: Any time of year, open from dawn to dusk

Pass/Permit/Fees: Free

Closest City or Town: Decatur, AL

How to Get There: From Decatur, head southeast toward Lee St. NE, turn right onto Lee St. NE. Take a sharp left onto 2nd Ave. NE, turn left onto Gordon Dr. SE, and you will reach your destination. 825 Gordon Dr. SE, Decatur, AL 35601

GPS Coordinates: 34.59833° N, -86.97403° W

Did You Know? The park itself is full of rich history as it was built in 1887 in hopes of "re-inventing" the city of Decatur.

Point Mallard Park

Point Mallard Park is a waterpark that has operated for over 50 years! While there are lifeguards on staff, it is important to keep a close eye on your children at all times, especially while in the water. Point Mallard Park offers several different events throughout the year, such as swim time with the mermaids. At the park, there are several different amenities like miniature golf, campgrounds, and even ice skating rinks! Bike trails, batting cages, and park pavilions are available, as well as an amphitheater for up to 75 guests.

Best Time to Visit: During the warmer months of the year

Pass/Permit/Fees: Adults (Age 12-61): $20, Children (Ages 5-11) and Seniors (62+): $15, Children under 4: Free

Closest City or Town: Decatur, AL

How to Get There: From Decatur, head southeast toward Lee St. NE, turn right onto Lee St. NE, and turn right at the first cross street onto Ferry St NE. Turn right onto Church St. NE, take a slight right onto 19th Ave. SE, continue onto Point Mallard Dr. SE, turn right toward 8th St. SE/Point Mallard Cir. SE. Take a slight right onto 8th St. SE/Point Mallard Cir. SE, turn right, turn left, and you'll reach 2901 Point Mallard Dr. SE, Decatur, AL 35601

GPS Coordinates: 34.57156° N, -86.93474° W

Did You Know? Some of the park's attractions are temporarily closed, so be sure to call for details if you are planning to use amenities such as the ice skating rink.

The Princess Theatre

The Princess Theatre has remained a popular destination in Decatur, Alabama, for more than 100 years. In 1887, this location was used as a stable where people kept their horses. It became a playhouse in 1919.

In 1949, after several renovations, the theatre was made to look as it does today and drew in performers from all over the country. The Princess Theatre was renovated another time and was reopened as Decatur's performing arts center, seating 677 guests.

Best Time to Visit: Any time of year

Pass/Permit/Fees: Cost of the concert or show you are attending

Closest City or Town: Decatur, AL

How to Get There: From Decatur, head southeast toward Lee St. NE, turn right onto Lee St. NE. Take a sharp left onto 2nd Ave. NE and turn left onto Holly St. NE. The destination will be on the right. 112 2nd Ave. NE, Decatur, AL 35601

GPS Coordinates: 34.60544° N, -86.98481° W

Did You Know? When the Princess Theatre was renovated in 1941, it was in Art Deco style and includes a bright neon sign on the outside of the building.

Wheeler Lake

Wheeler Lake is found in the northern part of Alabama and is made along the Tennessee River by Wheeler Dam. For 60 miles, this lake extends across the land, marking it as the second largest lake in the entire state.

Each year, Wheeler Lake has over 4 million visitors that come to fish, boat, and camp around the area. While visiting the lake, there is no swimming or wading allowed as an alligator nest is said to exist in the water.

Best Time to Visit: Any time of year

Pass/Permit/Fees: Free

Closest City or Town: Decatur, AL

How to Get There: From Decatur, head southeast toward Lee St. NE, turn right onto Lee St. NE. Turn right at the first cross street onto Ferry St. NE, turn right onto Vine St. NE, turn left onto US-31 N/6th Ave. NE. Continue to follow US-31 N, continue straight onto US-31 N/US-72 ALT E. Keep left to continue on US-31 N, turn left onto Thomas L Hammons Rd., continue onto Harris Station Rd. Continue straight onto Bridgeforth Rd. Turn left onto Beulah Bay Rd., turn left, and you will arrive at your destination.

GPS Coordinates: 34.76827° N, -87.05001° W

Did You Know? Another reason you are not able to swim in this water is that there are very high levels of pollution in the lake—so high that it is considered dangerous to swim.

Wheeler National Wildlife Refuge

Wildlife Refuges are great places to observe nature and find endangered species in the area. Wheeler National Wildlife Refuge offers just this with a plethora of outdoor activities to enjoy. By limiting the hours and areas where hiking is permitted, the wildlife is protected.

The hours of operation vary for different times of the year. From November-February, it is open seven days a week, 9 a.m.-5 p.m. every day. The hours from March-October are from 9 a.m.-4 p.m., and they are closed on Sunday and Monday each week.

Best Time to Visit: Early spring

Pass/Permit/Fees: Free

Closest City or Town: Decatur, AL

How to Get There: From Decatur, head northwest toward Ferry St. NE, turn left onto Ferry St. NE, turn left onto Lee St. NE. Turn right onto 6th Ave. NE (pass the Sonic), turn left onto Point Mallard Pkwy., turn right onto Visitors Center Rd, and your destination will be on the right.

Wheeler National Wildlife Refuge Visitor Center, 3121 Visitor Center Rd., Decatur, AL 35603

GPS Coordinates: 34.54774° N, -86.95114° W

Did You Know? The Wheeler National Wildlife Refuge runs along 20 miles of the Tennessee River.

Bankhead National Forest

Bankhead National Forest covers 181,230 acres and is one of four national forests in Alabama. Nicknamed the "Land of 1,000 Waterfalls," the Bankhead National Forest is a beautiful and enjoyable piece of nature in the northwest part of the state.

While visiting the forest, guests often enjoy canoeing, boating, fishing, swimming, horseback riding, hiking, and camping. The center of the forest is in Montgomery and was established as a national forest in 1918.

In addition to the numerous waterfalls, the Bankhead National Forest includes limestone bluffs, streams, and wildlife at just about every turn you make.

Best Time to Visit: Spring through early summer when the rain is present to fill creeks and waterfalls

Pass/Permit/Fees: $3 per vehicle

Closest City or Town: Double Springs, AL

How to Get There: From Double Springs, head west on Blake Dr. toward AL-195 S, turn right onto AL 195-N, turn left onto US-278 W, and you will arrive at your destination. Bankhead National Forest, 1070 AL-33, Double Springs, AL 35553

GPS Coordinates: 34.22837° N, -87.35079° W

Did You Know? The Bankhead National Forest is home to several white-tailed deer, gray and fox squirrels, waterfowl, raccoons, rabbits, turkeys, quail, and many more species!

Town of Spectre Movie Set

In Millbrook, Alabama, you'll find the well-known small town that was created for the filming of the movie *Big Fish*, commonly known as "Town of Spectre." This movie set is still standing for guests to visit, as the crew simply left the buildings upon completion of the film.

There are some parts of the set that are no longer able to be explored by tourists and guests; for example, Jenny's home located on the river was flooded and had to be torn down. Many people enjoy adding a pair of shoes to the line when they visit the Town of Spectre Movie Set.

Best Time to Visit: Any time of year

Pass/Permit/Fees: $3 per person

Closest City or Town: Elmore County, AL

How to Get There: Drive east on Cobbs Ford Rd./Alabama River Pkwy. for 3.5 miles. After crossing the train tracks, turn left onto Cypress Lane. When you arrive at the gate, call the posted phone number for the gate code, pay your fee, and follow Cypress Lane across the bridge to Spectre, AL.

GPS Coordinates: 32.44918° N, -86.32879° W

Did You Know? In the movie *Big Fish*, Spectre is a symbol for "the most heavenly place."

White Cliffs of Epes

The White Cliffs of Epes are found along the Tombigbee River in Epes, Alabama. These cliffs are along the sides of the river and are a photo-worthy stop while visiting the state. The cliffs are formed as a part of the Selma Chalk formations.

The steep walls of White Cliffs stretch for one mile, and as time goes on, they become more and more exposed due to the rushing water. They stand about 30 feet above the water, making them very easy to see and observe. This natural beauty is something that Alabama residents claim "everyone must see at least once in their lifetime."

Best Time to Visit: Any time of year, but not during rain as it might be difficult to observe the natural beauty

Pass/Permit/Fees: Free

Closest City or Town: Epes, AL

How to Get There: From Epes, head south on Minus St. toward US-11 S, turn left onto US-11 N, and you will reach your destination. White Cliffs of Epes, 26867 US-11, Epes, AL 35460

GPS Coordinates: 32.69552° N, -88.11587° W

Did You Know? These chalk formations were developed around the same time as the White Cliffs of Dover in England.

Walls of Jericho

The Walls of Jericho include mountains, springs, caves, rocky bluffs, grass coves, and woods that span over 25,000 acres of land. As it's a part of the North Alabama Birding Trail, guests can observe many different bird species at this location.

In addition to bird watching, camping and hiking are popular adventures for guests as the area has an 11-mile horseback riding trail and several areas to hike as well.

Along the hike are several photo-worthy scenic areas, including a beautiful waterfall and blue pool. Previous hikers have deemed this hike to be "difficult," so make sure you have the proper shoes before beginning your adventure.

Best Time to Visit: March through November

Pass/Permit/Fees: Free

Closest City or Town: Estillfork, AL

How to Get There: From Estillfork, head west on County Rd. 9 toward County Rd. 519, turn left onto AL-146 E, turn left onto AL-79 N. Turn left at Bear Den Point Loop Trail, and you will arrive at your destination.

GPS Coordinates: 34.98293° N, -86.07890° W

Did You Know? The name "Walls of Jericho" was given by John Robert Kennamer, Sr., who discovered it in the 1800s. He claimed only a biblical name would come close to describing the beauty and splendor of this site.

Eufaula National Wildlife Refuge

Eufaula National Wildlife Refuge is located in two states: Alabama and Georgia. This 11,184-acre refuge protects several species and has more than 4,000 acres of water. In addition, there are also many acres of wetlands, woodlands, grasslands, and croplands within the wildlife refuge.

The diversity of the area adds to the beauty and charm as it has a variety of different animals and birds that take shelter here every year. While you are allowed to take a boat out on the water for fishing, it is important to note that there are copperheads and alligators in the area, so always be cautious and aware of your surroundings.

Best Time to Visit: Any time of year

Pass/Permit/Fees: Free

Closest City or Town: Eufaula, AL

How to Get There: From Eufaula, head east on E Barbour St. toward S Randolph Ave., turn left onto N Randolph Ave., turn left onto St James Pl. Turn right at the first cross street onto N Eufaula Ave., turn right onto AL-165 N, and you will arrive at your destination.

GPS Coordinates: 32.01118° N, -85.09022° W

Did You Know? The Eufaula National Wildlife Refuge protects very rare species, including the wood stork.

Dauphin Island

Dauphin Island is a quiet, beautiful beach located on the Gulf of Mexico. The significance of this island lies in its rich historic Fort Gaines, which was used during the Civil War. The fort is available for exploration from guests as it overlooks the Gulf of Mexico and Mobile Bay. The island is a highly sought-after tourist destination for families looking to escape the hustle and bustle of everyday life. Dauphin Island does not have much to offer as far as shopping (the island does not even have a single traffic light) but will instead provide white sand beaches, nature trails, and relaxation.

Best Time to Visit: April-mid May, September-early November

Pass/Permit/Fees: To enter Dauphin Island, guests must pay $6 to park a car. The walk-in fee is $2 per person, and RVs/buses/trailers will cost $20.

Closest City or Town: Fairhope, AL

How to Get There: To get to Dauphin Island, travelers can cross over the 3-mile-long Dauphin Island Bridge on I-193. If you prefer to take a ferry, it will cost about $16, depending on your vehicle size. The ferry leaves every 1.5 hours between the hours of 8 a.m.-7 p.m. During inclement weather, the ferry will not be available for travelers.

GPS Coordinates: 30.25483° N, -88.10488° W

Did You Know? Dauphin Island is home to one of the biggest bird sanctuaries, spanning 164 acres.

Weeks Bay National Estuarine Research Reserve

The Weeks Bay National Estuarine Research Reserve (NERR) is home to many fish and bird species. At this location, research is done to learn more about each bird and fish in the habitat, as well as more information on the 6,000+ acres of land it includes. The Weeks Bay NERR is the perfect location for visitors who love to observe birds. The Pitcher Plant Bog Trail is also available to allow for hiking and is easy to follow. At the Weeks Bay National Estuarine Research Reserve, you will witness the location where the river and the ocean meet.

Best Time to Visit: March-April is when the flowers are blooming, and there are many birds to observe

Pass/Permit/Fees: Free

Closest City or Town: Fairhope, AL

How to Get There: From Fairhope, head east on Eastern Shore Trail/Fairhope Ave. toward N Section St., turn right at the first cross street onto S Section St., turn left onto Old Battles Rd. Turn right onto US-98 E/S Greeno Rd., turn left onto US-98 E, turn right, and you will reach your destination. Weeks Bay National Estuarine Research Reserve, 11300 US-98, Fairhope, AL 36532

GPS Coordinates: 30.41935° N, -87.83053° W

Did You Know? The reserve has both saltwater and freshwater marshes.

W.C. Handy Home and Museum

In the center of Florence, Alabama, is the W.C. Handy Home and Museum, where you can visit the W.C. Handy Cabin, visit the library and explore the museum. Handy was a "Father of the Blues" from Florence, born in a log cabin (that you can observe) in 1873.

At this museum are collections of Handy's personal papers, artifacts, and memorabilia from his life. The piano that was played with the St. Louis Blues is here for guests to view as well as hand-written sheet music from W.C. Handy himself.

Best Time to Visit: Any time of year

Pass/Permit/Fees: $5-$12 per ticket

Closest City or Town: Florence, AL

How to Get There: From Florence, head southeast on N Pine St. toward W Tennessee St., turn right at the second cross street onto W College St. Continue straight to stay on W College St., turn right, take a slight right and turn left. Your destination will be on the left. 620 W College St., Florence, AL 35630

GPS Coordinates: 34.79612° N, -87.68520° W

Did You Know? William Christopher Handy (W.C. Handy), nicknamed the "Father of the Blues," was the first person to write and publish blues music.

DeSoto Falls

DeSoto Falls is the most popular waterfall in Alabama, and for a good reason! These falls are 107 feet tall and exceptionally beautiful as the colors change in the autumn months of the year.

To reach the falls from the parking lot, it will require a short hike down 50 steps to reach the overlook. Once you reach the waterfall, there are several areas to eat a picnic lunch and admire the beauty of the falls. If there is not any rain, there won't be much water to fall down the waterfall.

Best Time to Visit: Spring, late fall, and winter (falls are dry in summer months)

Pass/Permit/Fees: Free

Closest City or Town: Fort Payne, AL

How to Get There: From Fort Payne, head northeast on Gault Ave. N toward 5th St., turn right at the first cross street onto 5th St. Turn left onto Wallace Ave. NE, turn left onto Desoto Pkwy. NE, continue onto Lookout Mountain Pkwy., turn left at CR 89. Turn right onto CR 89/ Desoto Pkwy., turn right onto CR 613, continue to Desoto Falls Rd. Continue to 613, and your destination will be on the right.

GPS Coordinates: 34.55038° N, -85.59073° W

Did You Know? This waterfall can be difficult to find because, during times of drought or little rainfall, the falls do not flow!

Little River Canyon National Preserve

Located close to Fort Payne, Alabama lies the Little River Canyon National Preserve. This 15,288-acre preserve includes the longest river on top of mountains in the United States. The Little River Canyon National Preserve was previously in the southern part of the DeSoto State Park before becoming a national preserve. To hunt or fish in this area, you must have a hunting and/or fishing license, but camping and riding ATVs are not allowed. There is a scenic drive that includes 23 miles of breathtaking views along the Little River Canyon Rim Parkway, as well as three waterfalls and many miles of trails to hike and explore.

Best Time to Visit: Weekdays and in fall or spring to avoid large crowds

Pass/Permit/Fees: Free

Closest City or Town: Fort Payne, AL

How to Get There: From Fort Payne, head northeast on Gault Ave. N toward 5th St., turn right at the first cross street onto 5th St. Turn left onto AL-35 S/Wallace Ave. NE and continue until you reach the destination. Little River Canyon National Preserve, 4322 Little River Trail #100, Fort Payne, AL 35967

GPS Coordinates: 34.38858° N, -85.62533° W

Did You Know? The Little River is the only river that extends and runs its entire length through the top of a mountain and became a national preserve in 1992.

Noccalula Falls Park

Noccalula Falls Park provides outdoor adventures and memories for the entire family. With a 90-ft drop, this waterfall flows into the Black Creek Ravine in Gadsden, Alabama. The park has many amenities to offer guests, such as a petting zoo, numerous plants to observe in botanical gardens, a miniature train, picnic pavilions, gift shop, playgrounds, miniature golf (for a separate fee), campgrounds, swimming pools, and cabins. The Black Creek Trail includes 1.7 miles of scenic landscapes, starting at the famous Noccalula Falls Wedding Chapel.

Best Time to Visit: Visit after a rainstorm when the waterfall is at its fullest.

Pass/Permit/Fees: Adults: $6 per visit, Children/Seniors: $4 per visit, Children 3 and Under: Free. Miniature Golf rates — Adults: $5, Children/Seniors: $4, Groups (10+): $3.50

Closest City or Town: Gadsden, AL

How to Get There: From Gadsden, head northeast on S 6th St. toward Broad St., turn left onto W Meighan Blvd., take a slight right onto N 12th St. Continue onto Noccalula Rd/Woodliff Rd., turn left onto Mann Dr., turn left, and your destination will be on the left. Noccalula Falls, Gadsden AL 35904

GPS Coordinates: 34.04319° N, -86.02074° W

Did You Know? The botanical gardens in the Noccalula Falls area have over 25,000 azaleas.

Bon Secour National Wildlife Refuge

"Bon Secour" literally means "safe harbor," which tells you everything you need to know about Bon Secour National Wildlife Refuge. This is a place for animals to be protected and live without fear of being hunted. In this wildlife refuge are many endangered creatures, from birds to mice to other unique creatures. The refuge is also a living laboratory, available for both scientists and students to study and further learn about the animals and plants that are in this area.

Best Time to Visit: Summer, but always bring water, so you do not get dehydrated on the hiking trails. Only service dogs are allowed on the trails

Pass/Permit/Fees: Free

Closest City or Town: Gulf Shores, AL

How to Get There: From Gulf Shores, head north toward W Beach Blvd., turn right on W Beach Blvd., turn left onto W 6th St. Continue onto Windmill Ridge Rd., turn left onto Gulf Shores Pkwy., continue on this road and pass by NAPA Auto Parts. Turn left onto AL-180 W/W Fort Morgan Rd., and you will arrive at your destination. Bon Secour National Wildlife Refuge, 12295 AL-180, Gulf Shores, AL 36542

GPS Coordinates: 30.24109° N, -87.82461° W

Did You Know? Along the trails, you will find many reptiles, including lizards, snakes, turtles, and possibly even alligators!

Fort Morgan State Historic Site

During the War of 1812, Fort Bowyer was used for military purposes. Between the years of 1819-1833, the fort was rebuilt and opened as Fort Morgan, which played a key role in the Battle of Mobile Bay. As the years passed, this fort was continually used in other wars, such as the Spanish-American War, WWI, and WWII. When you visit the Fort Morgan State Historic Site, you will gain so much knowledge and appreciation of the history that happened right at this location. There are also boat lunches offered, picnic areas, and beaches for guests to enjoy. The Fort is located at the very end of Gulf Shores Hwy. 180, so keep driving until the road ends!

Best Time to Visit: Any time of year

Pass/Permit/Fees: Adults: $8, College Students/Seniors/Children (6-12): $5

Closest City or Town: Gulf Shores, AL

How to Get There: From Gulf Shores, head north toward W Beach Blvd., turn right onto W Beach Blvd., turn left onto W 6th St., continue onto Windmill Ridge Rd. Turn left onto Gulf Shores Parkway. Continue straight to stay on Gulf Shores Pkwy. (Pass NAPA Auto Parts - Autoworx LLC on the right), turn left onto AL-180 W/W Fort Morgan Rd./Fort Morgan Rd. and you will reach your destination.

GPS Coordinates: 30.23040° N, -88.01636° W

Did You Know? People usually plan for two hours when taking a self-guided tour of Fort Morgan.

Gulf Shores

One of the most well-known and visited beaches in Alabama is Gulf Shores. The white sands are beautiful and relaxing for families to enjoy time away. There is always a variety of wildlife and many family-friendly activities for everyone to enjoy.

Along the coast in Gulf Shores are many restaurants, hotels, and condos for guests to have direct beach access from a number of different locations. There are certain times of year that are hurricane season, so coming in early fall or early spring are the best times to visit.

Best Time to Visit: Early fall (September-October) and Early spring (April-May)

Pass/Permit/Fees: Free

Closest City or Town: Foley, AL

How to Get There: From Foley, head south on N McKenzie St. toward Alabama's Coastal Connection/W Laurel Ave., continue straight onto S McKenzie St (pass by Centennial Bank on the left). Continue straight onto AL-59 S/S McKenzie St. (pass by TCBY on the right), turn right onto Windmill Ridge Rd. Continue onto W 6th St., turn right onto W Beach Blvd., turn left, and you will arrive at Gulf Shores, AL.

GPS Coordinates: 30.2460° N, -87.7008° W

Did You Know? Gulf Shores is commonly referred to as "Pleasure Island," a name given by Jim Folsom.

Borden Creek

Borden Creek is located within the Sipsey Wilderness and Bankhead National Forest. At the creek, there is a trail, often said to be poorly marked, so come with a map or GPS to help you navigate the area.

At Borden Creek, guests are able to enjoy hiking, biking, camping, hunting, and fishing. The entire Borden Creek trail is 2.7 miles in length and is a bit challenging in areas.

Best Time to Visit: Any time of year

Pass/Permit/Fees: $5 per person

Closest City or Town: Haleyville, AL

How to Get There: From Haleyville, head north on 11th Ave. toward 20th St. (pass by McDonald's on the left), turn right onto AL-195 S/21stSt. Turn left onto Kinlock Rd. Turn right onto Cranal Rd., continue onto Co. Rd. 6, turn left onto AL-33 N, turn left toward Restricted Northwest Rd., turn left toward Restricted Northwest Rd. Continue onto NW Rd., continue onto Mountain Springs Rd., continue onto Restricted Mountain Springs Rd.

GPS Coordinates: 34.37242° N, -87.36060° W

Did You Know? To reach the waterfall, you must hike 4.9 miles, but it is well worth the effort!

Sipsey Wilderness Area

Across Northwestern Alabama run many creeks that all flow into the Sipsey River. In the 24,922-acre wilderness are caves, overlooks, sinkholes, and trails that are there to help guests navigate their way through the area. Guests often use the Sipsey Wilderness Area as a great location for camping, hunting, and fishing. Some trails even allow you to explore via horseback. A common occurrence in the Sipsey Wilderness Area is waterfalls as a result of the limestone and sandstone layers. Some have even referred to the area as the "Land of 1,000 Waterfalls."

Best Time to Visit: Winter. People have reported that there are fewer bugs and more manageable temperatures

Pass/Permit/Fees: $3 Recreation use fee

Closest City or Town: Haleyville, AL

How to Get There: From Haleyville, head north on 11th Ave. toward 20th St. (pass McDonald's on the left), turn right onto AL-195 S/21st S.t and follow to AL-195 S. Turn left onto Co. Rd. 93, turn right onto Co. Rd. 92, continue to Co. Rd. 303. Take a slight right at Co. Rd. 1, another slight right onto Co. Rd. 303, followed by another right onto NW Rd., and you will arrive at your destination. Sipsey Wilderness, Mt. Hope, AL 35651

GPS Coordinates: 34.32925° N, -87.46819° W

Did You Know? The Sipsey Wilderness Area is the first designated wilderness east of the Mississippi River.

Aldridge Gardens

The 30-acre Aldridge Gardens were opened in 2002 to the public and showcase the horticulturists Eddie and Kay Aldridge. Here you will find hydrangeas along with many other flower and plant species.

The garden offers art exhibits, classes, bird walks, days for fishing, and other events. Guests can visit the couple's previous home as well as enjoy an outdoor pavilion, education building, and a half-mile walking trail around the 5-acre lake on the garden property.

Best Time to Visit: Any time of year, 8 a.m.-7 p.m., unless it is raining. Closed on Thanksgiving Day, Christmas Eve, Christmas Day, New Year's Day, and for special events, so check for availability before visiting.

Pass/Permit/Fees: Free, as this is a self-guided tour

Closest City or Town: Hoover, AL

How to Get There: From Hoover, head south on Whispering Pines Cir. toward Spruce Dr., turn right onto Spruce Dr., turn left onto Braddock Dr. Continue straight and turn right onto Lorna Rd., turn left, turn left, turn right, and you will reach your destination. 3530 Lorna Rd, Hoover, AL 35216

GPS Coordinates: 33.38857° N, -86.79117° W

Did You Know? At the Aldridge Gardens, Kay Aldridge patented the Snowflake Hydrangea. In 1997, the couple conveyed the gardens with the lake and walking trail to the City of Hoover.

Moss Rock Preserve

The Moss Rock Preserve is full of so much nature and has forests, large rocks, streams, waterfalls, wildlife, and so much more! Visiting the Moss Rock Preserve is a must-do item if you are in this part of the state.

The Moss Rock Preserve has six very rare species of plants that are hardly found anywhere else in the world. If you like to climb rocks, then seeing the Boulder Field will be something you do not want to miss. The area offers 12 miles of hiking trails as well.

Best Time to Visit: Any time of year

Pass/Permit/Fees: Free

Closest City or Town: Hoover, AL

How to Get There: From Hoover, head west on Deo Dara Dr., turn left to stay on this road. Turn right onto Hummingbird Ln., turn left onto Burning Tree Dr. Turn right onto Patton Chapel Rd., continue on Chapel Rd., turn left onto Preserve Pkwy, and turn right to stay on this road. At the traffic circle, take the first exit, and your destination will be on the right. 617 Preserve Way, Hoover, AL 35226

GPS Coordinates: 33.38157° N, -86.83983° W

Did You Know? The Moss Rock Preserve covers over 349 acres of land with boulders that guests can climb on and enjoy.

Sougahoagdee Falls

Observing waterfalls is always something that many visitors find to be breathtaking and worth the effort. Sougahoagdee Falls is located close to Houston, Alabama, and has hiking trails for all different skill levels.

To reach the waterfall, you must first hike four miles; several nature trips are offered to help get you there. If you want to bring a dog, you are allowed to, as long as you keep it on a leash.

This waterfall is considered Alabama's most beautiful waterfall, and many people find that once arriving at the falls, after a hike, it is well worth the effort and time.

Best Time to Visit: Spring

Pass/Permit/Fees: Free

Closest City or Town: Houston, AL

How to Get There: From Houston, head north on Co. Rd. 63, turn left onto US-278 W, turn right onto Co. Rd. 63. Turn right onto Hickory Grove Rd., and your destination will be on the left. Sougahoagdee Falls Parking, Hickory Grove Rd, Houston, AL 35572

GPS Coordinates: 34.25143° N, -87.24571° W

Did You Know? While it is a four-mile hike to the actual waterfall, there are several smaller waterfalls along the way, which helps make the hike more exciting and enjoyable.

Alabama Constitution Village

At the Alabama Constitution Hall Park, guests can see what life used to be like in 1819. The Alabama Constitution Village includes historical buildings that show what Huntsville looked like during the time of the Constitutional Convention in 1819.

The 90-minute guided tour teaches guests how Alabama became a state and shows how people survived during those days. With several different artifacts, children ages 12+ can learn how a printing press worked as well as observe other historical items.

Best Time to Visit: Any time of year, but the attraction is currently closed

Pass/Permit/Fees: Unknown

Closest City or Town: Huntsville, AL

How to Get There: From Huntsville, AL, head northeast on Spring St. SW toward Jefferson St. S (Spring St. SW turns right and becomes West Side Square). Continue onto Madison St. SE, turn left onto Gates Ave. SE and your destination will be on the left. 109 Gates Ave. SE, Huntsville, AL 35801

GPS Coordinates: 34.73040° N, -86.58318° W

Did You Know? This historical open-air museum reenacts daily life during the 1800s and includes a print shop, post office, cabinetmaker's shop, and law office.

Big Spring Park

Big Spring Park is located in Huntsville, Alabama, and is a key location for many events and festivals. At this park, young children can enjoy the ducks, koi, and geese. Many people are also drawn to the cherry trees that surround the red bridge in the park.

Big Spring was the original water source that brought water to the city. The park is soon to be the starting point for the 70-mile-long bike or hiking trail known as the Singing River Trail of North Alabama.

Best Time to Visit: May, as the temperatures are in the 80s and there are light rain showers

Pass/Permit/Fees: Free

Closest City or Town: Huntsville, AL

How to Get There: From Huntsville, head northeast on Spring St. SW toward Jefferson St. S (this road will turn into West Side Square). Turn right onto Fountain Cir. SW and the destination will be on the right. 420 Church St. NW, Huntsville, AL 35801

GPS Coordinates: 34.72975° N, -86.58605° W

Did You Know? This park is located in the heart of Huntsville, making it accessible and easy to find.

Bridge Street Town Centre

At the Bridge Street Town Centre in North Alabama, guests can enjoy shopping, food, and events. This outdoor shopping mall features stores, restaurants, and a movie theater for your entertainment as well.

Many people enjoy the shops here, but there are also pop-up events throughout the year that draw guests to the area. All of your shopping and entertainment needs can be met here at the Bridge Street Town Centre.

Best Time to Visit: Any time of year

Pass/Permit/Fees: Free

Closest City or Town: Huntsville, AL

How to Get There: From Huntsville, head southwest on Spring St. SW towards Spragins St. SW (Spring St. SW turns right and becomes Spragins St. SW). Turn right onto Monroe St. NW, turn left onto Washington St. NW, turn left to merge onto I-565 W. Take Exit 14B toward AL-255 N/Research Park Blvd, merge onto AL-255/Research Park Blvd. NW, take the Madison Pike exit. Keep right at the fork and merge onto Madison Pike, turn right onto Governors W, turn right, and you will reach your destination. 365 The Bridge St. #106, Huntsville, AL 35806

GPS Coordinates: 34.71852° N, -86.67377° W

Did You Know? The Bridge Street Town Centre features more than 70 shops and restaurants!

Burritt on the Mountain

Burritt on the Mountain has a historical park that shows different aspects of life on the farm from the Tennessee Valley. There are living history interpreters who are dressed in clothing of the period and recreate life on a farm for guests to enjoy.

Guests are welcome to walk through the park and soak up the sounds, views, and history that are available at Burritt on the Mountain. The interpreters are there to answer any questions you might have about the time period, and if you listen closely, you might even hear a banjo playing.

Best Time to Visit: Any time of year

Pass/Permit/Fees: Adults: $12, Children and Students: $8, Seniors and Military: $10, Children under 2: Free

Closest City or Town: Huntsville, AL

How to Get There: From Huntsville, head northeast on Spring St. SW toward Jefferson St. S (Spring St. SW turns right and becomes West Side Square). Continue onto Madison St. SE and pass by the Regions Bank on the right. Turn left onto Governors Dr. SE, turn left onto Monte Sano Blvd. SE, turn left onto Burritt Dr. SE, and your destination will be on the left. 3101 Burritt Dr. SE, Huntsville, AL 35801

GPS Coordinates: 34.71591° N, -86.53973° W

Did You Know? The house of William Henry Burritt has 14 bedrooms and is built in the shape of an X.

Historic Huntsville Depot

The Historic Huntsville Depot is the oldest railroad depot in the state and one of the oldest in the entire country. During the Civil War, this railway was used as a strategic point for holding Confederate soldiers, and their graffiti on the walls is still visible to this day.

Today, the depot is used as a museum with a 0-4-0 Porter steam locomotive, originally from Pittsburgh in 1904, located out front. While visiting the museum, guests are free to climb on the locomotive and explore several hands-on activities.

Best Time to Visit: Any time of year

Pass/Permit/Fees: The depot is $15 and $5 for each of the additional buildings you would like to explore.

Closest City or Town: Huntsville, AL

How to Get There: From Huntsville, head southwest on Spring St. SW toward Spragins St. SW (Spring St SW turns right and becomes Spragins St. SW). Turn left onto Clinton Ave. W, turn right onto Church St. NW, and the destination will be on the right. Huntsville Depot Museum, 320 Church St. NW, Huntsville, AL 35801

GPS Coordinates: 34.73467° N, -86.59084° W

Did You Know? The Depot was used as a Union hospital, a prison for Union soldiers, and was a key location for the Civil War.

Huntsville Botanical Garden

The Huntsville Botanical Garden consists of 112 acres of beautiful botanical grounds located in Huntsville, Alabama. Here, guests can explore the butterfly house, observe several different species of flowers and trees, and enjoy the outdoors. The garden is divided into several different sections: the nature center, which overlooks Little Smith Lake; the biblical garden with plants mentioned in the Bible; and the central corridor with an aquatic garden, daylily garden, dogwood trail, fern glade, herb garden, nature trail, and vegetable garden.

Best Time to Visit: Any time of year; hours of operation are Monday-Saturday: 9 a.m.-5 p.m., Sunday from 11 a.m.-5 p.m.

Pass/Permit/Fees: Adults: $14, Military/Student/Seniors (55+): $12, Children 3-17: $9, Children 2 and under: Free

Closest City or Town: Huntsville, AL

How to Get There: From Huntsville, head southwest on Spring St. SW toward Spragins St. SW (Spring St. SW turns right and becomes Spragins St. SW). Turn left onto Clinton Ave. W, turn left onto Triana Blvd. SW, turn right onto Bob Wallace Ave. SW. Turn left, and you will arrive at your destination. 4747 Bob Wallace Ave. SW, Huntsville, AL 35805

GPS Coordinates: 34.70738° N, -86.63373° W

Did You Know? The Huntsville Botanical Gardens have some of the most diverse ecosystems in Alabama.

Madison County Nature Trail

The Madison County Nature Trail is a beautiful trail that allows guests to explore the wilderness any time of the year. From azaleas and dogwoods in the springtime to colorful wildflowers in the summer, each season has something spectacular to offer.The nature trail is 1.5 miles long, and along the way, you will have access to a pavilion, chapel, outdoor classroom, restrooms, and more. If you are looking for a great place to fish, then you will find that here as well, for a small fee of $3.

Best Time to Visit: Any time of year

Pass/Permit/Fees: $3 fishing fee

Closest City or Town: Huntsville, AL

How to Get There: From Huntsville, head northeast on Spring St. SW toward Jefferson St. S (Spring St. SW turns right and becomes West Side Square). Continue onto Madison St. SE (pass by Regions Bank on the right) and continue onto Whistleburg Dr. Turn left onto Airport Rd. SE (Airport Rd. SE turns slightly right and becomes Carl T Jones Dr. SE), continue onto Bailey Cove Rd. SE, turn left onto Green Mountain Rd. SE. Turn right onto Shawdee Rd. SE, turn right onto Nature Trail Rd. SE and you will arrive at your destination. 5000 Nature Trail Rd. SE, Huntsville, AL 35803

GPS Coordinates: 34.59816° N, -86.51748° W

Did You Know? The park where this nature trail is located is on top of Green Mountain.

Merrimack Hall Performing Arts Center

The Merrimack Hall Performing Arts Center is found in Huntsville, Alabama, and is a 25,000-square-foot building built in 1898 and originally known as the Merrimack Hall. In 1920, the building was expanded and became a central hub of life in Huntsville.

Alan and Debra Jenkins purchased the hall in 2006, had about $2.5 million in renovations done, and reopened it to the public in 2007 as a 300-seat performance hall. Merrimack Hall has a Happy HeARTs program that caters to intellectually and physically challenged individuals. Over time, the hall has given over $1.5 million back to the community through various outreach programs it offers.

Best Time to Visit: Any time of year

Pass/Permit/Fees: Ticket prices vary with performances

Closest City or Town: Huntsville, AL

How to Get There: From Huntsville, head southwest on Spring St. SW toward Spragins St. SW (Spring St. SW turns right and becomes Spragins St. SW). Turn left onto Clinton Ave. W, turn left onto Triana Blvd. SW (pass by Subway) and the destination will be on the right. 3320 Triana Blvd SW, Huntsville, AL 35805

GPS Coordinates: 34.70454° N, -86.60947187224743° W

Did You Know? The Merrimack Hall originally only offered one-week-long dance classes for ten children with special needs before growing into the outreach center it is today.

Monte Sano State Park

The Monte Sano State Park is found in Northeastern Alabama, close to Huntsville. The breathtaking views have brought people to the area since the 1800s as a place to relax and take in some fresh air.

With 14 cabins, public restrooms, meeting rooms, and a terrace, there is so much Monte Sano State Park has to offer, including 89 campsites! With 2,140 acres of land, there are several viewing locations from the top of the mountain and miles of hiking and biking trails for your enjoyment.

Best Time to Visit: Any time of year, but the fall colors and spring blooms are noteworthy

Pass/Permit/Fees: Adults/Ages 12+: $5, Seniors/Ages 4-11: $2, Active military: $2

Closest City or Town: Huntsville, AL

How to Get There: From Huntsville, head northeast on Spring St. SW toward Jefferson St. S (this road turns right and will become West Side Square), continue on Madison St. SE (pass by the Regions Bank on the right). Turn left onto Governors Dr. SE, turn left onto Monte Sano Blvd. SE, turn right onto Nolen Ave. SE and you will arrive at your destination.

GPS Coordinates: 34.74000° N, -86.51187° W

Did You Know? The name "Monte Sano" in Spanish means "Mountain of Health."

North Alabama Railroad Museum

Located east of Huntsville lies the North Alabama Railroad Museum, where you will learn so much about the history of railroads and trains. There are several options for a self-guided walking tour, but there are also guided tours offered. In the center of the museum is the Chase Depot, one of the smallest union depots in the U.S. The North Alabama Railroad Museum offers train rides, three locomotives for you to tour and explore, as well as other equipment that was used to make the railroad system possible.

Best Time to Visit: Any time of the year

Pass/Permit/Fees: Self-guided tours are free. Rides are $20 for regular passengers and $30 for first-class.

Closest City or Town: Huntsville, AL

How to Get There: From Huntsville, head southwest on Spring St. SW toward Spragins St. SW (Spring . SW turns right and becomes Spragins St. SW), turn right onto Monroe St. NW. Turn left onto Washington St. NW, turn right to merge onto I-565 E, and merge onto I-565 E. Continue onto Hwy. 72 E/Lee Hwy. Turn left onto Moores Mill Rd. NE, turn left onto Chase Rd. NE and your destination will be on the left. 694 Chase Rd. NE, Huntsville, AL 35811

GPS Coordinates: 34.78498° N, -86.54252° W

Did You Know? The railroad is open for train rides that will take passengers over the Mercury and Chase Railroads.

Railroad Station Antique Mall

The building that the Railroad Station Antique Mall is found in has been in the National Registry of Historic Places since 1980. When the building was originally built in 1922, it was three stories high. Over time, the location has been different types of businesses — from a grocery store to a moving and storage company.

In 1983, the location was opened as the Railroad Station Antique Mall, where guests can shop and find one-in-a-million pieces of antiques or collectibles. The antique shop is located in the middle of downtown Huntsville, with several other must-see places around.

Best Time to Visit: Any time of ycar

Pass/Permit/Fees: Free

Closest City or Town: Huntsville, AL

How to Get There: From Huntsville, head southwest on Spring St. SW toward Spragins St. SW (Spring St. SW turns right and becomes Spragins St. SW). Turn right onto Monroe St. NW, turn right onto Jefferson St. N, and the destination will be on the right. 315 Jefferson St. N, Huntsville, AL 35801

GPS Coordinates: 34.73465° N, -86.58855° W

Did You Know? The prices here are very reasonable, and you can always find unique dishes, knickknacks, crafts, paintings, and more.

Twickenham Historic District

The Twickenham Historic District is found in Huntsville, Alabama, and features various architecturally styled homes from the year 1818. One of the most popular homes that people love to visit is that of poet and artist Maria Howard Weeden; here, you'll find the 1819 Weeden House Museum.

These antebellum homes that are there for guests to visit are beautiful and full of rich history. The city has guided and self-guided walking tours available.

Best Time to Visit: Any time of year

Pass/Permit/Fees: Visiting the historic district is free to the public, but the tours will cost money.

Closest City or Town: Huntsville, AL

How to Get There: From Huntsville, head northeast on Spring St. SW toward Jefferson St. S (Spring St. SW turns right and becomes West Side Square), continue onto Madison St SE, and turn left onto Williams Ave. SE. Take a slight right onto McClung Ave. SE and you will arrive at your destination.

GPS Coordinates: 34.72919° N, -86.57734° W

Did You Know? The Twickenham Historic District covers about 13 blocks of homes between the downtown and Maple Hill areas.

U.S. Space & Rocket Center

Another great location in Huntsville is the U.S. Space and Rocket Center, where you can explore several achievements, rockets, and artifacts from the U.S. Space program. Several astronauts have visited the museum and have said the U.S. Space and Rocket Center is "a great way to learn about space in a town that has embraced the space program from the very beginning." There are more than 1,500 artifacts, exhibits, and bus tours to the NASA Marshall Space Flight Center that is located nearby.

Best Time to Visit: Any time of year

Pass/Permit/Fees: $25 general admission for adults and children ages 13+. Children ages 5-12 are $17, and children under age 4 are free.

Closest City or Town: Huntsville, AL

How to Get There: From Huntsville, head southwest on Spring St. SW (Spring St. SW turns right and becomes Spragins St. SW), turn right onto Monroe St. NW. Turn left onto Washington St. NW, turn left and merge onto I-565 W. Take Exit 15 for Bob Wallace Ave., keep left toward Madison Pike, turn left onto Madison Pike (Madison Pike turns right and becomes Tranquility Base). Turn left to reach 1 Tranquility Base, Huntsville, AL 35805

GPS Coordinates: 34.71132° N, -86.65367° W

Did You Know? There are at least 12 astronauts who have graduated from the space camp offered at the U.S. Space and Rocket Center.

U.S. Veterans Memorial Museum

If you are looking for a place that proudly shows the accomplishments of American soldiers, then the U.S. Veterans Memorial Museum is a great place to visit. Here you will learn about WWI and see how the survivors and families lived during that time. The museum has over 30 historical military vehicles from World War I through the present day, allowing you to see how they've changed.

Best Time to Visit: Any time of year, Wednesday-Saturday

Pass/Permit/Fees: $16 for adults, $12 for students. For those with disabilities and members of the military, the cost is $14

Closest City or Town: Huntsville, AL

How to Get There: From Huntsville, head southwest on Spring St. SW (Spring St. SW turns right and becomes Spragins St. SW), turn left onto Clinton Ave W. Turn left onto the US-431 S ramp to US-231 S, continue onto US-431 S. Continue straight onto AL-53 S, take the left ramp to Huntsville High School. Merge onto US-231 S, take the Airport Rd. exit, merge onto S Memorial Parkway/US-231 Frontage Rd. Turn right onto Steve Hettinger Dr. SW, continue onto Old Airport Rd. SW, take two lefts, and you will reach 2060 Airport Rd. SW, Huntsville, AL 35801

GPS Coordinates: 34.69207° N, -86.58557° W

Did You Know? This museum holds 12,000 square feet of military memorabilia and artifacts.

Weeden House Museum

The Weeden House was built in 1819 and was owned by Dr. William Weeden and his family until 1956. The house was then purchased by the City of Huntsville and used in the Twickenham Historic Preservation District Association as a museum depicting a 19th century home.

Guided tours are available for a small fee, but the house is also available to rent for various events, such as weddings. This beautiful home is well-maintained and full of historical artifacts and architecture.

Best Time to Visit: Guided tours available Monday-Friday at 10 a.m. and 1 p.m.

Pass/Permit/Fees: Adults: $5, Children: $3, no debit or credit cards

Closest City or Town: Huntsville, AL

How to Get There: From Huntsville, head northeast on Spring St. SW toward Jefferson St. S (Spring St. SW turns right and becomes West Side Square), continue onto Madison St SE. Turn left onto Gates Ave. SE and your destination will be on the right. 300 Gates Ave. SE, Huntsville, AL 35801

GPS Coordinates: 34.73001° N, -86.58221° W

Did You Know? Behind the house is a garden that is beautifully laid out and landscaped, and guests are welcome to stroll through the garden as well as the house.

Barber Vintage Motorsports Museum and Park

The Barber Vintage Motorsports Museum and Park are where you can find the world's largest collection of motorcycles. This museum was built by George Barber and includes a 2.38-mile road course.

When visiting this track, many people are amazed at the beauty of the course. Several events are held here throughout the year, and it is commonly referred to as "The Augusta National of Motorsports."

Best Time to Visit: Any time of year

Pass/Permit/Fees: $15 per person, $10 for children

Closest City or Town: Leeds, AL

How to Get There: From Leeds, head west on Ashville Rd. NE toward Cogbill St. NE, turn right onto Parkway Dr (pass the Dollar General), turn left onto Rex Lake Rd. Turn right onto Barber Motorsports Pkwy., keep left, turn left at the first cross street, and you will arrive at your destination. 6030 Barber Motorsports Pkwy. Leeds, AL 35094

GPS Coordinates: 33.53366° N, -86.61402° W

Did You Know? At any point in time, there are over 900 motorcycles on display in the Barber collection at the museum.

Stephens Gap

Stephens Gap is one of the most loved caves in the country that includes a huge entrance and 143-foot cave. At Stephens Gap, a unique act of nature occurs where a waterfall falls into a cave. This incredible sight to see makes this a popular tourist destination for photographers and hikers. Alabama residents often refer to Stephens Gap as the most beautiful natural wonder in the entire state. To reach the cave itself, you must hike a 2-mile (round trip) trail first; always make sure you have the proper shoes, as the trail is known for being slippery. This site is privately owned property, but a free permit will grant you access to the natural beauty known as Stephens Gap.

Best Time to Visit: After a rainstorm, most commonly during the fall

Pass/Permit/Fees: You must have a permit to enter the cave, but it is free

Closest City or Town: Lim Rock, AL

How to Get There: From Lim Rock, head northwest on Co. Rd. 119 toward AL-35 S, turn right onto AL-35 N, turn right toward Co. Rd. 30. Turn left onto Co. Rd. 30, and your destination will be on the right. Stephens Gap Callahan Cave Preserve 8408 Co. Rd. 30, Woodville, AL 35776

GPS Coordinates: 34.67303° N, -86.21707° W

Did You Know? Stephens Gap is one of the most photographed cave entrances in North America.

Talladega Superspeedway

If you are a fan of NASCAR, then making a stop at the Talladega Superspeedway is a must-do item on your trip to Alabama. In addition to watching amazing racing take place, there is also a place to set up camp outside the track.

This speedway is the "biggest and baddest" track and one that race fanatics love to see and visit. One of the most legendary races held here is the Talladega 500, a 188-lap race that ends up being 500 miles long!

Best Time to Visit: Springtime is the best for races

Pass/Permit/Fees: Various packages are available to visitors

Closest City or Town: Lincoln, AL

How to Get There: From Lincoln, head west on 1st Ave. toward Magnolia St., turn left onto Magnolia St, take a sharp left onto US-78 E, turn right onto N Co. Rd. 399. Turn right toward North Blvd. and continue, turn left toward North Tunnel, turn right onto North Tunnel, continue onto Turn Four Lane. Turn right onto Road Course Loop, and the destination will be on the left. 3366 Speedway Blvd., Lincoln, AL 35096

GPS Coordinates: 33.56718° N, -86.06543° W

Did You Know? The total spectator capacity at the Talladega Superspeedway is 175,000.

Natural Bridge of Alabama

When it comes to natural beauty, Alabama is one of the most interesting and amazing places to visit. Observing the beautiful nature of the state is something many people love to do, and why stopping at the 60-ft tall, 148-ft long rock bridge is a must-see item. The Natural Bridge of Alabama is the largest natural bridge on the east side of the Rockies. Here, guests can enjoy the nature paths, stop for a picnic lunch, or visit the gift shop located nearby. Sadly, guests are no longer able to walk over the top of the bridge because, due to no side rails, it can be very dangerous. This bridge was labeled a national park in 1954, but the Native Americans used the bridge for many years previously.

Best Time to Visit: Any time of year; however, the springtime blooms and fall colors add to the experience

Pass/Permit/Fees: $3.50 per adult, $2.50 per child

Closest City or Town: Lynn, AL

How to Get There: From Lynn, AL, head northwest on Co. Rd. 59 towards Dodd St. Turn right onto Heck St. left onto AL-5 N, continue onto AL-13 N, turn left onto Co. Rd. 9, turn left to stay on Co Rd 9, and your destination is on the left.

GPS Coordinates: 34.09462° N, -87.61564° W

Did You Know? The Natural Bridge of Alabama is said to be more than 200 million years old. The bridge was used for shelter, and in the rocks, you can find a carving unlike any other in the entire world — of an Indian head.

Civil Rights Memorials of Montgomery

The Civil Rights Memorials of Montgomery have a black granite circular table that lists the martyrs of the Civil Rights Movement. Out of the center of this table flows water with an inscription of Martin Luther King, Jr.'s paraphrasing of Amos 5:24.

Guests are encouraged to physically touch the names engraved on the table to help them remember those killed during the movement and to reflect on how far the country has come since those days.

Best Time to Visit: Any time of year; Monday-Friday 9 a.m.-4:30 p.m., Saturday 10 a.m.-4 p.m.

Pass/Permit/Fees: Adults: $2, under 18: Free

Closest City or Town: Montgomery, AL

How to Get There: From Montgomery, head north on N Perry St. toward Madison Ave., turn right at the first cross street onto Madison Ave. Turn right onto S Decatur St, turn right onto Washington Ave., and your destination will be on the left. 400 Washington Ave., Montgomery, AL 36104

GPS Coordinates: 32.37628° N, -86.30267° W

Did You Know? Please check The Civil Rights Memorial Center website for temporary closures before planning a visit.

Montgomery Museum of Fine Arts

The Montgomery Museum of Fine Arts is home to over 4,000 artifacts, including American sculptures and paintings, art glass, and Old Masters prints. Several exhibits are made for hands-on educational purposes. Spanning more than 175-acres, the Montgomery Museum of Fine Arts is a great location for enjoying the Alabama Shakespeare Festival as well as the Hannah Daye Ridling Bark Park. Here you will find many miles of walking trails, an outdoor theatre, and breathtaking scenery.

Best Time to Visit: Any time of year

Pass/Permit/Fees: Free admission and parking

Closest City or Town: Montgomery, AL

How to Get There: From Montgomery, head on N Perry St. toward Madison Ave., turn right onto Madison Ave. Turn right onto S Decatur St., turn left onto Arba St. Take the ramp onto I-85 N, and merge onto I-85 N. Keep left to stay on I-85 N, take Exit 6 to merge onto US-231 S/US-80 W/Eastern Blvd. toward AL-21 S. Merge onto US-231 S/US-80 E/Eastern Blvd., turn left onto Woodmere Blvd, turn right onto Festival Dr. Turn left onto Museum Dr., turn right and your destination will be on the right. 1 Museum Dr., Montgomery, AL 36117

GPS Coordinates: 32.35196° N, -86.20648° W

Did You Know? The Montgomery Museum of Fine Arts was originally founded by local artists and called Alabama Society of Fine Arts.

Perry Lakes Park

Perry Lakes Park is located close to the Cahaba River and is home to many bald eagles at the entrance of the park. At this park are several architectural features created by the students from Auburn University. Included among these features are the 100-ft birding tower and the restroom facilities.

Perry Lakes Park includes a 1/4-mile trail that leads to Barton's Beach Cahaba River Preserve, which has a nice overlook over the river.

If you are following one of the Alabama Birding Trails, you will more than likely make a stop near Perry Lakes Park.

Best Time to Visit: Any time of year

Pass/Permit/Fees: Free

Closest City or Town: Marion, AL

How to Get There: From Marion, head east on Jefferson St. toward Washington St., continue onto AL-14 E/Martin Luther King Pkwy, continue to follow AL-14E. Take a slight left, take a slight left again onto AL-175 N, and your destination will be on the right. Perry Lakes Park, AL-175, Marion, AL 36756

GPS Coordinates: 32.69893° N, -87.25989° W

Did You Know? About 150 years ago, the Cahaba River changed its course, and that is when the oxbow lakes in the park were formed.

Jackson Lake Island

Jackson Lake Island is a popular tourist destination for the use of boats, fishing, and observing where Tim Burton's 2003 film, *Big Fish*, was made.

This small island has room for camping, picnic pavilions, bench swings, and a boat ramp for easy access. The waters around the island are very still, and people enjoy going canoeing here.

Jenny, from the movie *Big Fish*, still has remnants of her house that are visible from the lake's edge and the southern side of the island.

Best Time to Visit: Any time of year

Pass/Permit/Fees: $3 per person, children under age 2 are free. Camping costs are $10 per person and $5 for children.

Closest City or Town: Millbrook, AL

How to Get There: From Millbrook, head south on AL-143 S/Main S.t toward Frasier St. (pass by Kwik Shop on the right). Turn left onto Alabama River Pkwy., turn left onto Cypress Ln, and you will arrive at your destination.

GPS Coordinates: 32.45022° N, -86.33735° W

Did You Know? Jackson Lake Island is privately owned but open to the public for a small fee.

Cathedral-Basilica of the Immaculate Conception

The Cathedral-Basilica of the Immaculate Conception is the first Catholic Church on the Gulf Coast, established in 1703. The City of Mobile was founded in 1702, and shortly after, this Catholic cathedral was built. The church was rebuilt in 1711 and was given the title Cathedral-Basilica of the Immaculate Conception in 1781.

Guests are welcome to tour the cathedral but keep mindful of the daily mass times. Many guests come to observe the beautiful stained-glass windows that were originally installed in 1890. The church has gone through several disasters, including a Union Army ammunition depot exploding in 1865, which killed 300 people, and a fire in 1954.

Best Time to Visit: Daily mass schedule Monday-Friday: 12:10 p.m., Saturday: 8 a.m. Visitors are welcome any time, but please remain mindful of daily mass times.

Pass/Permit/Fees: Free

Closest City or Town: Mobile, AL

How to Get There: From Mobile, head west on St Louis St., turn left onto N Clairborne St., and the destination will be on the right. 2 S Clairborne St., Mobile, AL 36602

GPS Coordinates: 30.69115° N, -88.04534° W

Did You Know? The Cathedral-Basilica of the Immaculate Conception is the oldest religious congregation in Alabama.

Condé-Charlotte Museum House and the Bragg-Mitchell Mansion

Another one of the famous historic homes open to visitors is the Conde-Charlotte Museum House and the Bragg-Mitchell Mansion located in Mobile, Alabama. Here, guests can observe the grace and elegance of this beautiful mansion and learn more about the period in which it was originally built.

The mansion is available to be rented out for weddings or other functions. The Old South is perfectly represented by the mansion and allows people to remember the way of life and socialization from that time period.

Best Time to Visit: Any time of year

Pass/Permit/Fees: Adults: $10, Ages 6-12: $5, under 5: Free

Closest City or Town: Mobile, AL

How to Get There: From Mobile, head south on N Water St. toward Michael S.t, continue straight onto S Water St., take a slight right onto Water St. turn right onto Monroe St., turn right at the first cross street onto S Royal St., turn left onto Theatre St., and your destination will be on the right. 104 Theatre St., Mobile, AL 36602

GPS Coordinates: 30.68854° N, -88.03997° W

Did You Know? The Bragg-Mitchell Mansion was built in 1855 and is a really neat place to tour to learn about the time period and rich history of Alabama.

Fort Conde

The Colonial Fort Conde was originally built by French explorers in 1723. Over time, the fort was given several different names, such as Fort Louis, Fort Charlotte, and Fuerte Carlota. When the fort was rebuilt several years ago, it was added as part of the USA bicentennial celebration in 1976.

When you visit the History Museum of Mobile, you also get admission costs covered to visit Fort Conde. Many people visit these two places at the same time to save both money and time.

Best Time to Visit: Any time of year; open from M-S 9 a.m.-4:30 p.m. and Sunday from 1 p.m.-4 p.m.

Pass/Permit/Fees: Included in admission for History Museum of Mobile

Closest City or Town: Mobile, AL

How to Get There: From Mobile, head south on N Water St. toward St. Michael St., continue straight onto S Water S.t, take a slight right onto Water St. Turn right onto Church St., turn left at the first cross street onto S Royal St., and your destination will be on the right. 150 S Royal St., Mobile, AL 36602

GPS Coordinates: 30.69065° N, -88.03974° W

Did You Know? Since part of the fort was removed due to it not being needed any longer, it left the cannons at the site aimed at the high-rise buildings in Mobile.

Gulf Coast Exploreum Science Center

The Gulf Coast Exploreum Science Center provides hands-on educational exhibits for children and adults to help increase scientific knowledge in the Gulf Coast region. For about 35 years, this science center has been known to spark the imagination and curiosity to help people grow.

Throughout the year, various exhibits are brought to the Gulf Coast Exploreum Science Center, helping to keep the "young and young-at-heart" involved in learning. The science center has been a key field trip destination for students during the school year, so always check the calendar before you arrive to make sure the crowds are what you expect.

Best Time to Visit: Any time of year; Tuesday-Saturday 10 a.m.-4 p.m., closed on Sunday and Monday

Pass/Permit/Fees: Adult (13-64): $13, Youth/Senior (7-12/65+): $11, Children (3-6): $6

Closest City or Town: Mobile, AL

How to Get There: From Mobile, head south on N Water St. toward St Michael St., turn right onto St Francis St., turn left at the first cross street onto N Royal St. Turn left onto Government St. and the destination will be on the right. 65 Government St., Mobile, AL 36602

GPS Coordinates: 30.69124° N, -88.03661° W

Did You Know? The Exploreum Science Center is connected to the Poarch Band of Creek Indians Digital Dome Theater, where IMAX movies are shown.

GulfQuest National Maritime Museum of the Gulf of Mexico

The GulfQuest National Maritime Museum of the Gulf of Mexico is located in Mobile, Alabama, and serves as a way to educate the community. With hands-on activities for visitors, people can gain a deeper understanding of the Gulf of Mexico. The museum does have a few artifacts, but the main attraction at this location is the hands-on experiences. The more people can experience various things, the more likely they are to remember them, which is why this maritime museum exists. The building was started in 2010 and finally opened to the public in 2015.

Best Time to Visit: Any time of year; open Wednesday-Saturday 10 a.m.-4 p.m., closed Sunday-Tuesday

Pass/Permit/Fees: Adult: $10, Senior Adult: $8, Youth (Age 5-17): $6, Under 5: Free

Closest City or Town: Mobile, AL

How to Get There: From Mobile, head south on N Water St. toward St. Michael St., continue straight onto S Water St., take a slight right onto Water St. Turn left at Monroe St., take a sharp left, and the museum is on the right at 155 S Water St., Mobile, AL 36602

GPS Coordinates: 30.68920° N, -88.03753° W

Did You Know? The museum has more than 90 different hands-on exhibits and displays.

Mobile Carnival Museum

The Mobile Carnival Museum holds over 300 years of history from Mobile, Alabama. The main attraction at this museum is the celebration of Carnival and Mardi Gras in the city.

At the museum are several of the Queen's Gallery gowns, jewels, and other items worn by the queens of Carnival. There are several Mardi Gras posters, invitations, and other party items that are used in the celebration of these two events.

Best Time to Visit: Any time of year; open Monday, Wednesday, and Friday from 9 a.m.-4 p.m.

Pass/Permit/Fees: Adults: $8, Military/Students: $6, Children 12 and under: $3

Closest City or Town: Mobile, AL

How to Get There: From Mobile, head south on N Water St. toward St. Michael St., continue straight onto S Water St. Turn right onto Government St., and the destination will be on the left. 355 Government St., Mobile, AL 36602

GPS Coordinates: 30.68923° N, -88.04523° W

Did You Know? The artifacts saved and displayed in the Mobile Carnival Museum were all found in a period original, historic home.

Mobile Historic Districts

People who have visited Alabama have said that visiting the Historic Districts in Mobile is one of the most exciting and educational things you can do.

There are eight different districts, all with beautiful front porches, living rooms, and stunning landscaping. All of the displayed districts showcase a characteristic of the period of growth during the 19th and 20th centuries.

Best Time to Visit: Any time of year

Pass/Permit/Fees: Free

Closest City or Town: Mobile, AL

How to Get There: The historic districts are located all over the city. Here is a map showing each of the individual districts and how much land they cover.
https://maps.cityofmobile.org/pdf_maps/Overall%20Histori c%20Districts%20ARB.pdf

GPS Coordinates: 30.69479° N, -88.04345° W

Did You Know? The Mobile Historic Development Office is committed to saving buildings and neighborhoods to enrich the history of the area and educate visitors.

Mobile Museum of Art

The Mobile Museum of Art was founded in 1963 and showcases over 6,400 artifacts. The museum covers 95,000 square feet and has a lot to offer guests interested in art history.

The museum holds pop-up events throughout the city to increase community awareness of art history and works with other outreach programs to gain popularity and increase knowledge in the community.

Best Time to Visit: Open Tuesday-Saturday: 10 a.m.-5 p.m., closed Sunday-Monday and on all city holidays

Pass/Permit/Fees: Adults: $12, Seniors: $10, Students/Active Military: $8, Children under 6: Free

Closest City or Town: Mobile, AL

How to Get There: From Mobile, head east on St. Louis St. toward N Water St. turn left onto N Water St. Take a slight right onto the I-165 N/US-90 E ramp to US-98 E/US-43, continue onto I-165 N. Take Exit 1A on the left to merge onto I-65 S toward Mobile, take Exit 5A for Springhill Ave. Keep left at the fork and follow signs for Mobile Museum of Art/Gulf State Fairgrounds. Turn left onto Springhill Ave., turn left onto PFC John O New Dr., turn right onto Museum Dr., and your destination will be on the left. 4850 Museum Dr., Mobile, AL 36608

GPS Coordinates: 30.70530° N, -88.15427° W

Did You Know? The Mobile Museum of Art offers lectures and classes for children.

Mobile-Tensaw Delta

Alabama is home to the largest wetland ecosystem and second-largest river delta in the entire country, the Mobile-Tensaw Delta. A river delta occurs where a river meets a larger body of water, such as the ocean. At the Mobile-Tensaw Delta, there are 260,000 acres (40x10 miles) of wetland habitats in the form of lakes, ponds, sloughs, rivers, and creeks. With so much land to explore, several outdoor activities are available for your enjoyment and relaxation. From hunting and fishing to camping and canoeing, there is always something for everyone to have a good time at the Mobile-Tensaw Delta in Mobile, Alabama.

Best Time to Visit: Fall, as it is too cold for snakes this time of year!

Pass/Permit/Fees: Visiting the river delta is free; however, there are several boat tours and experiences available. https://wildnativetours.com/about-coastal-alabama/deltasafaris/

Closest City or Town: Mobile, AL

How to Get There: When you leave Mobile, drive North for 4 miles on US 43. Turn right onto Station Ave., and you will see the parking lot located on the left.

GPS Coordinates: 30.76667° N, -87.95227° W

Did You Know? The majority of the bodies of water that make up the Mobile-Tensaw Delta are too shallow for large boats, so most people enjoy taking kayaks or canoes out on the water.

Oakleigh Period Museum House

Built in 1833, the Oakleigh Period Museum House is located in the center of the Oakleigh Historic Complex, a group of buildings that have artifacts from the original time period. When the home was originally built, it was placed on 35 acres of land in Mobile by a man named James W. Roper. The surrounding clay pit was the reason for choosing the land where he used a Greek Revival style for the architecture of the house. The Museum House offers guided tours through the area to help enrich your knowledge and appreciation for the Oakleigh Period in Mobile, Alabama.

Best Time to Visit: Any time of year

Pass/Permit/Fees: Adults: $10, Students: $8, Children under 5: Free

Closest City or Town: Mobile, AL

How to Get There: From Mobile, head south on N Water St., continue straight onto S Water St., take a slight right onto Water St. Continue onto Canal St. Turn right onto S Washington Ave., turn left onto Government St., turn left onto George St., turn right onto Savannah St. Turn right onto Oakleigh Pl. and you will arrive at your destination. 300 Oakleigh Pl., Mobile, AL 36604

GPS Coordinates: 30.68319° N, -88.05499° W

Did You Know? The Oakleigh Period House Museum is located in the center of the Oakleigh Garden Historic District, minutes from the downtown area of Mobile.

Richards DAR House

In the heart of the De Tonti Square District lies the Richards DAR House, a very special landmark in Mobile, Alabama. This 10,000-square-foot home is full of period furniture and décor, including chandeliers, mantels, and staircases. Guests are welcome to come and tour the Richards DAR House and see where Captain Charles Richards and his bride Caroline Elizabeth Steele Richards used to live day to day in Mobile in the 1860s.

The venue is available to rent out for special events and is one of the most charming homes in the Old South. Guided tours are offered for those looking to learn even more about the home and time period.

Best Time to Visit: Any time of year, open Saturdays from 10 a.m.-4 p.m. and Sundays from 1 p.m.-4 p.m.

Pass/Permit/Fees: Adults: $10, Children (ages 5-12): $5, Children under 5: Free

Closest City or Town: Mobile, AL

How to Get There: From Mobile, head east on St. Louis St. toward N Water St., turn left onto N Water St. Take a slight left at Congress St. and continue onto Congress St. Turn left onto N Joachim St., and the destination will be on the left. 256 N Joachim St., Mobile, AL 36603

GPS Coordinates: 30.69661° N, -88.04474° W

Did You Know? There have been instances where people have reported seeing ghosts playing in the Richards DAR House Museum.

USS Alabama Battleship Memorial Park

The USS Alabama Battleship Memorial Park is located on the western shore of Mobile Bay. Here you can take a look at ships such as the South Dakota-class battleship, USS Alabama, and Gato-class submarine USS Drum. Some of the battleships in this memorial park are national historical landmarks, all offering information on the rich history of the ships. Education is a key purpose of this museum and memorial park.

Best Time to Visit: Any time of the week, open from 8 a.m.-5.p.m.

Pass/Permit/Fees: Age 55+: $13, Age 12-55: $15, Age 6-11: $6, Under 5: Free

Closest City or Town: Mobile, AL

How to Get There: From Mobile, head south on N Water St. toward St. Michael St., continue straight onto S Water St., take a slight right onto Water St. Turn right onto Church St., turn right onto S Jackson St. Turn right at the first crossroad to Government St., keep left on Government St. Take a slight right toward Old Spanish Trail, merge onto Old Spanish Trail, turn right and you will arrive at your destination. 2703 Battleship Pkwy., Mobile, AL 36603

GPS Coordinates: 30.68370° N, -88.01604° W

Did You Know? The USS Alabama is a battleship that has been retired but was the fourth and final member of the South Dakota class of first battleships built in the 1930s.

Moundville Archaeological Park

At the Moundville Archaeological Park, there are 326 acres where Native Americans built 28 flat-topped pyramids, all located around the central plaza building. These pyramids were used for ceremonies and housed the noblest of their tribes. The museum in the building has over 200 artifacts from the community. In addition, the park has a 0.5-mile nature trail that goes through the forest. Pack a picnic lunch so you can enjoy the Black Warrior River sites while you take a break and eat. This site is also on the West Alabama Birding Trail.

Best Time to Visit: Any time of year

Pass/Permit/Fees: Adults: $8, Seniors: $7, Children/Students: $6, Under 5: Free, Native Americans (with tribal membership card): Free

Closest City or Town: Moundville, AL

How to Get There: From Moundville, head north on Hwy. 69 for about 0.5 miles, turn west onto Mound Pkwy. Rd. Travel 0.4 miles, and you will arrive at the Park Entrance Building.

GPS Coordinates: 33.00294° N, -87.62809° W

Did You Know? Moundville Archaeological Park was founded by Native Americans from Mississippi and is one of the largest prehistoric Native American communities in the country.

Harmony Park Safari

The Harmony Park Safari is a nature preserve that showcases exotic and endangered species in Huntsville, Alabama. One feature of this nature preserve that people love is the fact that you can stay in your car!

This drive-thru safari is two miles long and allows you to see a variety of animals such as ostriches, giraffes, turtles, and buffalo. For safety reasons, no pets are allowed to come with you when you visit the animals.

Best Time to Visit: Spring; open from March-November

Pass/Permit/Fees: $10 per person

Closest City or Town: New Hope, AL

How to Get There: From New Hope, head east on Washington Ave. toward Main Dr. Turn left onto Main Dr. and continue on Old Hwy. 431. Turn left toward Hobbs Island Rd SE, turn right onto Hobbs Island Rd. SE, turn left onto Clouds Cove Rd. SE. Turn right to stay on Clouds Cove Rd. SE and your destination will be on the left. 431 Clouds Cove Rd. SE, Huntsville, AL 35803

GPS Coordinates: 34.53290° N, -86.47429° W

Did You Know? When you pay for your admission, you will be handed a bucket of animal food for you to feed the safari animals right from the comfort of your vehicle!

Flat Rock Park

Flat Rock Park is located close to Lake Wedowee and is commonly used as a location for soaking up the sun and fishing. This 25-acre spread of granite is used to attract visitors from near and far.

At the Flat Rock Park are picnic tables, grills, restrooms, fishing and swimming areas, and nature trails. Many people choose to paddle through the water to observe several coves and inlets along the way.

The Flat Rock Park overlooks Lake Wedowee and has a number of unique plants and wildlife in the area.

Best Time to Visit: May-September, 9 a.m.-8 p.m.

Pass/Permit/Fees: Free

Closest City or Town: Ofelia, AL

How to Get There: From Ofelia, head southwest on Co. Rd. 38 toward Co. Rd. 57, turn left onto Co Rd 57. Turn right onto AL-48 W, turn left onto Shady Grove Ln., turn left onto Blakes Ferry Rd. Continue straight on Co. Rd. 870 until you reach your destination.

GPS Coordinates: 33.33034° N, -85.62978° W

Did You Know? Even during the hottest times of the year, beautiful and colorful plants are still able to grow along the granite rock surfaces.

Splinter Hill Bog

There are 4.3 miles of trails that travel through the Splinter Hill Bog, allowing guests to enjoy and observe the unique plant species the state of Alabama has to offer. This destination is a stop along the Alabama Coastal Birding Trail.

Hunting is allowed on the property; however, you must have a valid license as well as a permit map.

The Splinter Hill Bog is closely managed and looked after by the nature preserve to protect the pitcher plants and other species in the area. When visiting this area, be sure to have a camera to capture its pure essence and beauty.

Best Time to Visit: The peak of pitcher blooming season is July-August, but in early spring, there are several beautiful flowers to see as well

Pass/Permit/Fees: Tours are $25 for garden members and $35 for non-members

Closest City or Town: Perdido, AL

How to Get There: From Perdido, head northwest on Co. Rd. 47 toward Co. Rd. 61, turn right onto Co. Rd. 61 and turn left onto Co. Rd. 47. Your destination will be on the left. Splinter Hill Bog, Co. Rd. 47, Bay Minette, AL 36507

GPS Coordinates: 31.02543° N, -87.68518° W

Did You Know? The Splinter Hill Bog is most commonly known for its plethora of carnivorous pitcher plants.

Dismals Canyon

In May of 1974, a sandstone gorge in Franklin County, Alabama, became a natural landmark. The canyon is home to several unique insects, most notably the dismalites (also known as *Orfelia Fultoni*), that are found covering the walls of the canyon. At Dismals Canyon, visitors can enjoy and observe two stunning waterfalls, Secret Falls and Rainbow Falls. Covering 85 acres of land, this nature-filled canyon offers a number of enjoyable activities for people of all ages. Many people choose to visit the canyon and camp, fish, and enjoy a nighttime tour to observe the unique insects that glow in the evening hours.

Best Time to Visit: April-May and September-October

Pass/Permit/Fees: Self-guided day tour: Adult-$12, Over 60-$11, under 12-$8.75. Guided Night Tour: Adult-$10, Over 60-$9, under 12-$7.75.

Closest City or Town: Phil Campbell, AL

How to Get There: Leaving Phil Campbell, head east on McClung Ave. towards Broad St., turn right at the first cross street onto Broad St. Turn right onto AL-237 S/Isom Ln., turn right onto College Rd., turn left onto US-43 S, turn right onto County Rd. 8, and Dismals Canyon will be on your left.

GPS Coordinates: 34.32631° N, -87.78148° W

Did You Know? The dismalites that glow in the evening hours are known to glow green and blue and are one of the biggest reasons why people visit the canyon.

Cooter's Pond Park

Off of the banks of the Alabama River lies Cooter's Pond Park, a frequently visited place by both people and birds. On the northern part of the park is a large wooded area, fields, picnic locations, and a view of the City of Montgomery. The southern part of the park has a river walk, picnic areas, and ramps for boats to enter the water.

Due to the location of the park, there are always several birds in this area, making it a big part of the Alabama Birding Trail. Many people report that this park "has it all" and that it is a must-see location if you are traveling through the state of Alabama.

Best Time to Visit: Any time of year

Pass/Permit/Fees: Free

Closest City or Town: Prattville, AL

How to Get There: From Prattville, head east on Wetumpka Rd. toward Pinecrest Rd., turn right onto S Memorial Dr., turn left onto Murfee Dr. Turn right onto Cooters Pond Rd., turn left to stay on Cooters Pond Rd. and your destination will be on the left. 1844 Cooters Pond Rd., Prattville, AL 36067

GPS Coordinates: 32.43287° N, -86.40187° W

Did You Know? The Cooter's Pond Park is beautiful at any time of the year and is dog friendly. This park is very clean, so all they ask is that you clean up after your pet!

Wilderness Park/Bamboo Forest

The Wilderness Park/Bamboo Forest is a beautiful destination that is dog friendly and includes a trail through the Bamboo Forest. In 1982, this was named the very first wilderness park in the United States.

In the Vietnam era, this forest was used by the U.S. military before it being named a wilderness park. The bamboo trees stand as high as 60 feet in the air, a sight that is hard to beat!

The trail at the park leads you through the trees, with 60-ft.-high trees on either side of the trail. The entire trail is manageable by most guests and is only 3/4 of a mile long.

Best Time to Visit: Any time of year

Pass/Permit/Fees: Free

Closest City or Town: Prattville, AL

How to Get There: From Prattville, head west on Wetumpka Rd. toward Pinecrest Dr., turn right onto N Northington St. Turn left at the first cross street onto E 6th St., turn right onto N Court St./Upper Kingston Rd. and your destination will be on the right. 800 Upper Kingston Rd., Prattville, AL 36067

GPS Coordinates: 32.47899° N, -86.48029° W

Did You Know? The Wilderness Park and Bamboo Forest is home to one of Alabama's largest beech trees.

Red Hills of Alabama

The Red Hills of Alabama stretch from the Mississippi River across the state of Alabama and into Florida as well. The hills are caused by the limestone and other sediments that have pushed upwards and created hills that rise to 510 feet above sea level.

This area is one of the most biologically diverse areas in North America, and here you can find more than 28 species of oak trees. Due to the unique nature of the area, some creatures are native only to this area, including the Red Hills Salamander.

The majority of guests to the Red Hills of Alabama are there to hunt, but there are also areas for camping as well.

Best Time to Visit: April-October

Pass/Permit/Fees: Free

Closest City or Town: Red Hill, AL

How to Get There: From Camden, take AL-41 S to River Ridge Rd. (22.2 miles), turn left on River Ridge Rd. and the parking lot will be on your left.

GPS Coordinates: 34.26038° N, -86.42268° W

Did You Know? The Red Hills Salamander is unique to the Red Hills of Alabama and is only found in this area. The largest Red Hills Salamander ever found was about 10 inches in length.

Joe Wheeler State Park

Joe Wheeler State Park is one of Alabama's 21 state parks, consisting of 2,550 acres of land. Here, guests can enjoy views, play an 18-hole golf course, enjoy a full-service marina, camp, rent a cottage or cabin, or hike the trails. This state park has the Tennessee River running down the center, making it a popular tourist destination for boating and fishing. Of all of the state parks in Alabama, the Joe Wheeler State Park is considered to be a "resort park," as it is very tourist-friendly and beautiful to visit. When the park is open, swimming is available in the bodies of water found in the Joe Wheeler State Park, but always proceed with caution as alligators have been seen in these areas.

Best Time to Visit: Any time of year when the park is reopened

Pass/Permit/Fees: Pricing is currently unavailable since the park is temporarily closed

Closest City or Town: Rogersville, AL

How to Get There: From Rogersville, head southeast on Lee St toward Wheeler St., turn right onto Wheeler St., continue onto Lambs Ferry Rd. Turn right onto Lover's Ln., turn right onto McLean Dr., and you will arrive at your destination. Joe Wheeler State Park, 4403 McLean Dr., Rogersville, AL 35652

GPS Coordinates: 34.81741° N, -87.34558° W

Did You Know? In 2019, a tornado ripped through the Joe Wheeler State Park and destroyed the camping area.

Neversink Pit

Neversink Pit is a cross between a sinkhole and a cave and is very commonly photographed and climbed. The opening at the top of the sinkhole is 40 feet in diameter and drops as much as 162 feet down to the floor of the cave.

Climbers have said that at any time of the year, the walls of the sinkhole are beautiful with ice, waterfalls, or ferns, depending on the time of year visited. To reach the bottom of the sinkhole, you must rappel and can only attempt it with a single rope technique.

Best Time to Visit: Any time of year

Pass/Permit/Fees: Permits are required but are free

Closest City or Town: Scottsboro, AL

How to Get There: From Scottsboro, head west toward E Peachtree St., turn right onto E Peachtree St., turn right onto S Broad St. Turn right at the second cross street onto AL-279 N/E Willow St., keep left at the fork, follow signs for Chattanooga and merge onto US-72 E/John T Reid Pkwy/Lee Hwy. Turn left onto Co. Rd. 42, and you will arrive at your destination in Fackler, AL.

GPS Coordinates: 34.79288° N, -85.91128° W

Did You Know? Neversink Pit is the most photographed pit in the Tennessee, Alabama, Georgia area due to the beautiful waterfall and fern-covered walls.

Unclaimed Baggage Center

One of the most unique places to shop is found in Scottsboro, Alabama, and is known as the Unclaimed Baggage Center. Here guests can shop for luggage, jewelry, electronics, and other various items from people who have not claimed their baggage while traveling.

When traveling, if a bag is lost, the owner has three months to claim all of their belongings. When a bag is left unclaimed, it is then sent to the Unclaimed Baggage Center and given a second life through selling, donating, and recycling. The store covers 50,000 square feet with merchandise and food as far as the eye can see! Many people find themselves leaving the store with great finds and even more amazing memories.

Best Time to Visit: Any time of year

Pass/Permit/Fees: Entrance is free; just pay for what you purchase

Closest City or Town: Scottsboro, AL

How to Get There: From Scottsboro, head west toward E Peachtree St., turn right onto E Peachtree St. Turn right at the second cross street onto Caldwell St., turn left onto W Willow St. and the destination will be on the left. 509 W Willow St., Scottsboro, AL 35768

GPS Coordinates: 34.67348° N, -86.04382° W

Did You Know? In the year 2016 alone, there were over 21.6 million lost or misplaced bags sent to the Unclaimed Baggage Center.

Weathington Park

Weathington Park is often used as a photo shoot location because of the spectacular views of the Tennessee River. When you stop to look over the river, the scenery extends for miles and miles.

The park covers about 13 acres of land and is often referred to as Alabama's "best-kept secret," as it is very quiet but beautiful. While Weathington Park is lovely at any point during the day, it is most spectacular when the sun is setting over the Tennessee River.

Best Time to Visit: Any time of year

Pass/Permit/Fees: Free

Closest City or Town: Scottsboro, AL

How to Get There: From Scottsboro, head west toward E Peachtree St., turn right onto E Peachtree St., turn right onto S Broad St. Turn right at the second cross street onto E Willow St., turn right onto AL-35 S/Veterans Dr., and you will be at your destination.

GPS Coordinates: 34.59196° N, -85.99961° W

Did You Know? The land where Weathington Park lies was donated in 2012 by Scott and Patty Weathington.

Lake Guntersville

Lake Guntersville is located in the northeastern part of Alabama and is found close to the Tennessee River. The park offers 6,000 acres of woodlands to explore with many exciting things to do.

Included at the location is an 18-hole championship golf course, zipline, beach complex, fishing in Alabama's biggest lake, outdoor nature center, and miles of hiking and biking trails that have guided hikes if needed. With 36 miles of hiking trails to explore, the Lake Guntersville area is set apart from all other parks in the state in that there are several opportunities to see bald eagles.

Best Time to Visit: For successful frog fishing, visit between late September and November

Pass/Permit/Fees: $5 per person

Closest City or Town: Section, AL

How to Get There: From Section, head south on Church St. toward Durham Dr. Church St. turns right and becomes Durham Dr. Turn left onto Main St. S, turn right onto Bluff Rd., continue onto Co. Rd. 265, turn right onto Langston Gap Rd. Turn left onto Co. Rd. 67/Langston Rd, take a slight right onto Davis Ln., turn right onto Davis Ferry Ln. Turn left onto Evans Rd, and you will arrive at your destination.

GPS Coordinates: 34.59913° N, -86.12721° W

Did You Know? The deepest part of Lake Guntersville is 60 feet deep!

National Voting Rights Museum and Institute

The National Voting Rights Museum and Institute was first established in 1991 as a place to honor and display artifacts from events leading up to the 1965 Selma to Montgomery marches as well as the 1965 Voting Rights Act.

Faya Ora Rose Toure and Marie Foster founded the museum and made the location close to the bridge where the marches originated. In the museum, guests can view the "Footsteps to Freedom" room that shows more detail of those time periods as well as a number of other artifacts.

Best Time to Visit: Any time of year

Pass/Permit/Fees: Adult: $6.50, Student: $4.50, Senior: $4.50

Closest City or Town: Selma, AL

How to Get There: From Selma, head northeast on Alabama Ave. toward Lauderdale St., turn right at the second cross street onto US-80 BUS. Turn right toward Cosby Ave., turn right onto Cosby Ave. and the destination will be on the right. 6 US-80 East, Selma, AL 36701

GPS Coordinates: 32.40329° N, -87.01625° W

Did You Know? The museum is located right next to the Edmund Pettus Bridge that was used on March 7, 1965, as a place where marchers met. This day was later known as "Bloody Sunday."

Alligator Alley

At Alligator Alley, guests will be taken through a guided or self-guided tour on an elevated platform overlooking over 200 alligators. The alligators are all different ages and stages; some will be relaxing, and others nesting. The tour includes a nature walk that shows the alligators in their natural habitat.

There are several hands-on experiences offered at Alligator Alley, all of which will leave you and your family with lasting memories.

Best Time to Visit: Any time of year; open 10 a.m.-5 p.m. daily; live feedings are at 11 a.m., 1 p.m., and 4 p.m.

Pass/Permit/Fees: Adults: $15, Seniors/Children (ages 3-12): $13, Toddlers (ages 2 and under): Free, Alligator chow: $5

Closest City or Town: Summerdale, AL

How to Get There: From Summerdale, head north on NE 1st St. toward E Jackson Ave., turn left at the first cross street onto E Jackson Ave. Turn right at the first cross street onto Co. Rd. 71/NW 1st St. Continue to follow Co. Rd. 71, and your destination will be on the right. 19950 Co. Rd. 71, Summerdale, AL 36580

GPS Coordinates: 30.51405° N, -87.69919° W

Did You Know? Alligators can grow up to a maximum length of 14 ft and can go up to 18 months without eating.

Bellingrath Gardens and Home

The Bellingrath Gardens and Home feature 65 acres of flowers at any point of the year. The home on the property is a 15-room house built in 1935 and is 10,500 square feet. The home has so much history to learn about, including the architecture and birthplace of Alva Smith Vanderbilt Belmont, a notable African American who was a major figure during the women's suffrage movement. The Bellingrath gardens bloom throughout the year, with each season bringing to life different kinds of flowers.

Best Time to Visit: Any time of the year

Pass/Permit/Fees: Adults: $22, Children (ages 5-12): $14, Children (under 4): Free

Closest City or Town: Theodore, AL

How to Get There: From Theodore, use Government Blvd./Spanish Trail to turn right onto Bellingrath Rd. Take a left on Co. Rd. 18, continue straight onto Bellingrath Gardens Rd., turn right, and you will reach your destination. 12401 Bellingrath Gardens Rd., Theodore, AL, 36582

GPS Coordinates: 30.43246° N, -88.14004° W

Did You Know? The home belonged to Walter and Bessie Bellingrath, one of the very first Coca-Cola bottlers in the Southeast. Due to his wealth and success, he was able to build this house and the gardens that surround it.

Children's Hands-on Museum

The Children's Hands-on Museum is a privately owned organization that was created in 1984 to help the youth of the city discover and learn more about their community and how they are a working part in the bigger picture.

Inside the museum is a Choctaw Indian Village, an interactive town including a general store, a bank, a hospital, and other shops for children to play in and learn more about. There is also a farm section including a farmers market, where children can play, learn, and grow—all while having fun.

Best Time to Visit: Any time of year; open Tuesday-Saturday: 9:30 a.m.-4 p.m.; closed on all major holidays and Sundays and Mondays

Pass/Permit/Fees: 65+ years: $8, 1-64: $9, Under 1: Free

Closest City or Town: Tuscaloosa, AL

How to Get There: From Tuscaloosa, head west toward 24th Ave/Greensboro Ave., turn right toward 24th Ave./Greensboro Ave., turn right onto 24th Ave/Greensboro Ave. Turn left at the first cross street onto University Blvd., and your destination will be on the right. 2213 University Blvd., Tuscaloosa, AL 35401

GPS Coordinates: 33.21032° N, -87.56589° W

Did You Know? In addition to several exhibits for children to play in, there is also a party room for people wanting to host birthdays.

Druid City Brewing Company

One of the most popular places to visit in Tuscaloosa is the Druid City Brewing Company. This brewing company recently merged with Straight to Ale and opened a larger location to accommodate guests. The restaurant has vinyl records playing during your visit, classic video games for guests to enjoy, and chalkboard paintings that alternate throughout the year. This location is full of culture and brews, so you can enjoy your Southern beverage in a fun location. Bands often play in the courtyard behind the brewing company, so always check the venue schedule to see who is playing when you come to visit and grab a beverage!

Best Time to Visit: Any time of year; open M-F from 4 p.m.-10 p.m. and Saturday-Sunday from noon-10 p.m.

Pass/Permit/Fees: No fee to visit

Closest City or Town: Tuscaloosa, AL

How to Get There: From Tuscaloosa, use University Blvd. to turn left onto Lurleen B. Wallace Blvd. S. Take the 15th St. ramp, keep left at the fork to continue toward 15th St. Turn left onto 15th St., turn left toward 14th St., turn right onto 14th, and your destination will be on the right. 607 14th St., Tuscaloosa, AL 35401

GPS Coordinates: 33.20155° N, -87.54525° W

Did You Know? The Druid City Brewing Company is a short walking distance from The University of Alabama, making it a popular college hang-out location.

Gorgas House Museum

The Gorgas House Museum was built in 1829 and is the oldest building on the campus of the University of Alabama. When it was originally built, its purpose was to be used as a dining hall and steward's place of residence. At the end of the Civil War, this was one of four buildings that were not destroyed in 1865. The museum is now home to original family memorabilia and other artifacts from 1879-1953. In 1971, the Gorgas House Museum was added to the National Register of Historic Places.

Best Time to Visit: Any time of year; M-F: 9 a.m.-12 p.m., 1-4:30 p.m., except for Wednesday mornings from 9-12 a.m.

Pass/Permit/Fees: Unknown

Closest City or Town: Tuscaloosa, AL

How to Get There: From Tuscaloosa, head west toward Greensboro Ave., turn right toward Greensboro Ave., turn left onto Greensboro Ave. Turn right onto Jack Warner Pkwy., turn right onto Hackberry Ln., turn right onto Margaret Dr. (Margaret Dr. turns right and becomes Capstone Dr.), and the destination will be on the right. 810 Capstone Dr., Tuscaloosa, Al 35487

GPS Coordinates: 33.21369° N, -87.54412° W

Did You Know? You are welcome to take a walk-in, self-guided tour, but if you call 205-348-5906 or email gorgashouse@ua.edu, you can reserve a spot in a 10-person guided tour.

Jemison-Van de Graaff Mansion

Jemison-Van de Graaff Mansion is an Italian mansion built in 1859-1862 that operates as a museum today. The home was built for Senator Robert Jemison, Jr. and his descendants.

After the Great Depression, this location became the public library, later, a publication office, and today is open as a museum. The museum shows the original decor and architecture and is a local landmark.

Best Time to Visit: Any time of year: Tuesday-Saturday at 3:30 p.m.

Pass/Permit/Fees: Free

Closest City or Town: Tuscaloosa, AL

How to Get There: From Tuscaloosa, head east toward University Blvd., turn right onto University Blvd. Turn left onto Lurleen B Wallace Blvd. S (pass by Jimmy John's on the left), take the 15th St ramp, keep left at the fork and continue toward 15th St. Turn left onto 15th St., and turn left onto 24th Ave./Greensboro Ave. and your destination will be on the right. 1305 Greensboro Ave., Tuscaloosa, AL 35401

GPS Coordinates: 33.20261° N, -87.56475° W

Did You Know? This mansion was the very first Italian-style home in the state of Alabama.

Lake Lurleen State Park

Lake Lurleen State Park is 1,625 acres of scenic views right off the edge of Lake Lurleen. Here, guests can experience ultimate relaxation and recreation — including over 23 miles of hiking trails. The park offers several facilities such as a campground, activity building, picnic area, playground, pavilions, beach access, fishing locations, RV storage, boat rentals, and 91 modern campsites.

Best Time to Visit: Any time of year

Pass/Permit/Fees: $4.75 non-refundable reservation fee, adults: $4, children/seniors: $1

Closest City or Town: Tuscaloosa, AL

How to Get There: From Tuscaloosa, head east toward University Blvd. and turn right. Turn right at the first cross street onto Hugh R. Thomas Bridge/Lurleen B Wallace Blvd. N, continue straight. Turn left onto McFarland Blvd, turn right onto US-43 N, turn left onto AL-171 N, turn left onto Eugenia Faucett Dr, turn left onto Shamblin Rd (Shamblin Rd turns slightly right and becomes Old Cove Rd.). Continue onto Shamblin Rd., continue straight, turn right onto Mt. Olive Rd., turn left onto Lake Lurleen Rd. 13226 Lake Lurleen Rd., Coker, AL 35452

GPS Coordinates: 33.30344° N, -87.67081° W

Did You Know? Lake Lurleen measures 1.5 miles in length, 0.5 miles wide, and is up to 48 feet deep. There are a ton of fish here to catch, including crappie, catfish, and bass.

Murphy-Collins House

The Murphy-Collins House was originally built in 1923 and sold to Sylvia Collins after being owned by the Murphys. Ms. Collins used the home to rent it out to the Phoenix House, a place for people recovering from alcoholism.

The Murphy-Collins Home is where the Murphy African American Museum is located, a place showcasing the history of African American life and culture in the Tuscaloosa, Alabama, area.

Best Time to Visit: Any time of year; Tuesday-Friday, call ahead to schedule a tour

Pass/Permit/Fees: Free

Closest City or Town: Tuscaloosa, AL

How to Get There: From Tuscaloosa, head east toward University Blvd., and turn right onto University Blvd. Turn left onto Lurleen B Wallace Blvd. S. Turn right onto 10th St./Paul W Bryant Dr., and the destination will be on the left. 2601 Paul W Bryant Dr., Tuscaloosa, AL 35401

GPS Coordinates: 33.20473° N, -87.56957° W

Did You Know? This museum shows the very important historical contributions of African Americans in Tuscaloosa during the 1920-1950 period.

Snow Hinton Park

In Tuscaloosa, Alabama, the Snow Hinton Park and provides an outdoor experience for children and adults. At the park are several picnic pavilions available for renting, multiple walking trails, a playground, and a jungle gym for the older children.

If you are looking to have a cookout at the park, electric grills and lighted athletic fields are available to the public. Public bathrooms and plenty of room to play and spend time outdoors are things you will find at Snow Hinton Park.

Best Time to Visit: Any time of the year, 7 a.m.-10 p.m. daily

Pass/Permit/Fees: Free

Closest City or Town: Tuscaloosa, AL

How to Get There: From Tuscaloosa, head west toward Greensboro Ave., turn right to Greensboro Ave., turn left onto Greensboro Ave., turn right onto Jack Warner Pkwy. Take the ramp onto US-82 E/McFarland Blvd. W, turn left, turn right, turn left toward 10th Ave. E. Turn right toward 10th Ave. E and the destination will be on the right.

GPS Coordinates: 33.18854° N, -87.52412° W

Did You Know? The Snow Hinton Park is located on one of the busiest roads in the downtown Tuscaloosa area, next to a grocery store and a seafood restaurant.

The Paul W. Bryant Museum

While many museums in Alabama focus on the history of the state and the movements that brought it to where it is today, The Paul W. Bryant Museum features a different type of memorabilia. Sports fanatics will find this museum a dream come true as it has several archives and exhibits honoring sports stars of the past. This museum is located very close to the University of Alabama and traces the history of its football team. Several players are showcased, and videos are shown to highlight specific plays and moments that brought them fame and helped the team.

Best Time to Visit: Any time of year; Tuesday-Sunday from 9 a.m.-4 p.m.

Pass/Permit/Fees: Adult: $5, Children (K-12): $3, Under 5: Free

Closest City or Town: Tuscaloosa, AL

How to Get There: From Tuscaloosa, head west toward 24th Ave./Greensboro Ave., turn right toward 24th Ave./Greensboro Ave., turn right again. Continue straight to stay on 24th Ave./Greensboro Ave., turn left onto 10th St./Paul W. Bryant Dr. Continue to follow this street, and your destination will be on the left. 300 Paul W. Bryant Dr., Tuscaloosa, AL 35401

GPS Coordinates: 33.20677° N, -87.53972° W

Did You Know? There is a gift shop at the museum for guests to purchase University of Alabama gear and clothing.

Tuscaloosa Farmers' Market

Stopping by the farmers' market is enjoyable and delicious for guests from all over. The ability to find locally grown produce is something many people enjoy doing and helps support local farmers and artisans.

In addition to produce, the Tuscaloosa Farmers' Market also has grass-fed meats, artisan crafts, and a great experience for anyone at any time of the year.

Best Time to Visit: Saturday year-round, also seasonal pop-up markets April-September

Pass/Permit/Fees: Free to enter, pay for what you want to purchase

Closest City or Town: Tuscaloosa, AL

How to Get There: From Tuscaloosa, head west toward Greensboro Ave., turn right onto Greensboro Ave. Turn left onto Greensboro Ave., turn right onto Jack Warner Pkwy. Make a U-Turn at River Rd. Condominium and your destination will be on the right. 1900 Jack Warner Pkwy., Tuscaloosa, AL 35401

GPS Coordinates: 33.21787° N, -87.56328° W

Did You Know? The Tuscaloosa Farmers Market is located along the banks of the Black Warrior River and draws many people to the area each year.

Cane Creek Canyon Nature Preserve

Cane Creek Canyon Nature Preserve is a privately-owned, 700-acre nature preserve with an 8.2-mile hiking trail. Even though this nature preserve is privately owned, it is open to the public at any time during the day for exploration and enjoyment. On the nature preserve, there are waterfalls, creeks, rock shelters, and fields. If you choose to hike through the Cane Creek Canyon Nature Preserve, expect to find scenic overlooks, wildflowers, pioneer cabin sites, and other unique sites.

Best Time to Visit: February-October

Pass/Permit/Fees: Free

Best Time to Visit: Friday-Sunday 7 a.m.-5 p.m.

Closest City or Town: Tuscumbia, AL

How to Get There: From Tuscumbia, head east on E 6th St. toward S Dickson St., turn right at the first cross street onto S Dickson St. Continue onto S Woodmont Dr. (pass AutoZone Auto Parts), turn right onto US-72 W/Lee Hwy., take a slight left. Turn left onto Frankford Rd., turn right onto Loop Rd., continue straight, take a slight right, and your destination will be on the left. Cane Creek Canyon Nature Preserve, 251 Loop Rd., Tuscumbia, AL 35674

GPS Coordinates: 34.62339° N, -87.79324° W

Did You Know? Unlike the other nature preserves in Alabama, this one is privately owned and open to the public free of charge. The owners are Jim and Faye Lacefield.

Tuscumbia's Spring Park

Tuscumbia's Spring Park is found in the northwest corner of Alabama and can offer events for your entire family. The Park is known for hosting festivals, events, and even some concerts.

In the evening hours, many visitors enjoy the water show and eliminated waterfall. At any point during the year, guests are allowed to fish for trout for a fee.

Tuscumbia's Spring Park also has a lake that provides the city with water to drink. Guests are also welcome to enjoy shelter from the sun, public restrooms, playgrounds, barbeque grills, power outlets, and the world's largest man-made stone waterfall.

Best Time to Visit: Any day of the year

Pass/Permit/Fees: Free

Closest City or Town: Tuscumbia, AL

How to Get There: From Tuscumbia, head east on E 6th St. toward S Dickson St., turn right at the first cross street onto S Dickson St. Turn right onto Spring Park Rd., and your destination will be on the left.

GPS Coordinates: 34.72929° N, -87.70407° W

Did You Know? About 4,320,000 gallons of water pass through the waterfall every single day.

Pinhoti National Recreation Trail

The Pinhoti National Recreation Trail is an excellent destination for visitors looking for different hiking challenges and adventures. This trail is found throughout the Talladega National Forest in Eastern Alabama. In addition to all of the nature this trail offers, there is also quite a bit of history to learn about along the way.

As you travel the trail, you will find mountain streams and forests, as well as 170 miles of things to discover and explore in the great outdoors. The entire trail extends to the surrounding states and is a total of 337.1 miles in length.

Best Time to Visit: Spring

Pass/Permit/Fees: Free

Closest City or Town: Unity, AL

How to Get There: From Unity, head north toward Coosa CR 56, turn left onto Coosa CR 56, turn left onto CR 55, turn left. Continue to CC Camp Rd, turn left, and your destination will be on the left.

GPS Coordinates: 32.97944° N, -86.35238° W

Did You Know? These trails stretch from Georgia to Alabama, so when you prepare to visit and want to hike the entire distance of the trail, be sure to schedule about 2-3 weeks to complete the hike.

Rickwood Caverns State Park

The Rickwood Caverns State Park was discovered in the 1950s, reopened to the public in 1974 as a state park, and is 380 acres of caverns to explore and discover. In addition to the guided cave tour, the caverns also have a hiking trail, gift shop, gemstone mining, camping, playground, Olympic-sized swimming pool, and a kiddie pool. The water is very cool because it's fed from underground.

Best Time to Visit: The caverns are enjoyable any time of year

Pass/Permit/Fees: Entrance Fees — Ages 5-11: $2, 12+: $3, Cave Tours (includes entrance fee) — Ages 5-11: $9, 12+: $19, Swimming (includes entrance fee) — Ages 5+: $7

Closest City or Town: Warrior, AL

How to Get There: From Warrior, head north on Bluff St. and turn right onto 2nd St., turn right onto Kemp Dr, turn left onto Caldwell Dr. Turn left onto Main St. N, continue straight onto Lester Doss Rd., turn right onto Skyline Dr, turn right onto Rickwood Caverns Rd. Turn right onto Rickwood Park Rd., and you will arrive at your destination. 370 Rickwood Park Rd., Warrior, AL 35180

GPS Coordinates: 33.87498° N, -86.86200° W

Did You Know? The caverns were discovered by Eddie Rickles and Sonny Arkwood in the 1950s while exploring with a Boy Scout troop. They combined their names and called it Rickwood Caverns.

Cahaba River National Wildlife Refuge

The Cahaba River National Wildlife Refuge was created as a means to preserve and protect wildlife in Alabama. The river itself flows through about 200 miles of Alabama land and is home to numerous wildlife and rare plant species.

In 2002, the Cahaba River National Wildlife Refuge was established due to the presence of a rare plant species called the *Hymenocallis Coronaria*, more commonly referred to as the Cahaba lily. With the refuge in place, this plant, along with others and any wildlife in the area, are protected and preserved. Visiting the Cahaba River National Wildlife Refuge will allow guests the opportunity to fish, canoe, hike, and take photos.

Best Time to Visit: Fall, when the colors of the leaves are changing

Pass/Permit/Fees: Free

Closest City or Town: West Blocton, AL

How to Get There: From I-20/59 take Exit 97. Follow Hwy. 11 3 miles south, turn left onto Hwy. 5 until CR 24. On CR 24, drive about 6 miles, and you will find the river access on the right side of Bibb County Rd. 24.

GPS Coordinates: 33.11360° N, -87.05759° W

Did You Know? If the area has experienced a lot of rain recently, be very cautious when entering the river as there is no staff on-site, and it can be very dangerous in some situations.

Wetumpka Impact Crater

Located in the city of Wetumpka, Alabama, is a natural phenomenon known as the Wetumpka Impact Crater. Many years ago, a meteor came crashing through the atmosphere and hit this town. As one of the only above-ground craters in the entire country, many people enjoy exploring the area. When this meteor hit the surface, it is believed to have sent shock waves and debris for hundreds of miles and even into the Gulf of Mexico.

Stretching 3-4 miles wide, the Wetumpka Impact Crater is hard to miss and very interesting to observe.

Best Time to Visit: Any time of year

Pass/Permit/Fees: Free

Closest City or Town: Wetumpka, AL

How to Get There: From Wetumpka, head south on N Broad St. towards W Tallassee St., turn left onto W Tallassee St. Turn right at the third cross street onto N Bridge St., turn left onto W Bridge St. (this will become S Main St.), turn left onto Ready St. Turn right onto Old US Hwy. 231, and your destination will be on the right. Wetumpka Impact Crater Marker, 6246-6422 AL-21, Wetumpka, AL 36092

GPS Coordinates: 32.5343° N, -86.20375° W

Did You Know? The meteorite that made this was estimated to be 1,100 feet across and came in from space at a 30-45-degree angle.

Cathedral Caverns State Park

The Cathedral Caverns were previously known as the "Bat Cave" when it was originally opened to the public in the 1950s. In the summer of 2000, the cave became a state park. With a gigantic entrance, people are wowed by the vast diversity of the caverns and the comfortable 60-degree weather year-round.

Cathedral Caverns State Park spreads out over 493 acres of land and even includes an outdoor hiking trail. Cave tours are enjoyable and educational for all ages and a must-see item in Alabama.

Best Time to Visit: Any time of the year as it is always about 60°F inside the caverns

Pass/Permit/Fees: Cave Tour rates: Ages 13+: $20, Ages 5-12: $9, Ages 4 and below: Free, Military Rate (with ID): $18

Closest City or Town: Located in Woodville, AL, about 30 minutes from Huntsville, AL

How to Get There: From Woodville, follow College St. onto Cathedral Caverns Hwy. for 2 miles. Turn left onto Cathedral Caverns Rd. and follow for about 3 miles. Turn right onto Cave Rd. and just shy of two miles down the road are the caverns.

GPS Coordinates: 34.57394° N, -86.22170° W

Did You Know? The Cathedral Caverns is home to "Goliath," one of the largest stalagmites in the entire world; it measures 45 feet tall and 243 feet in circumference.

Proper Planning

With this guide, you are well on your way to properly planning a marvelous adventure. When you plan your travels, you should become familiar with the area, save any maps to your phone for access without internet, and bring plenty of water—especially during the summer months. Depending on the adventure you choose, you will also want to bring snacks and even a lunch. For younger children, you should do your research and find destinations that best suits your family's needs. Additionally, you should also plan when to get gas, local lodgings, and where to get food after you're finished. We've done our best to group these destinations based on nearby towns and cities to help make planning easier.

Dangerous Wildlife

There are several dangerous animals and insects you may encounter while hiking. With a good dose of caution and awareness, you can explore safely. Here is what you can do to keep yourself and your loved ones safe from dangerous flora and fauna while exploring:

- Keep to the established trails.
- Do not look under rocks, leaves, or sticks.
- Keep hands and feet out of small crawl spaces, bushes, covered areas, or crevices.
- Wear long sleeves and pants to keep arms and legs protected.
- Keep your distance should you encounter any dangerous wildlife or plants.

Do not rely on cell service for navigation or emergencies. Always have a map with you and let someone know where you are and for how long you intend to be gone, just in case.

First Aid Information

Always travel with a first aid kit with you in case of emergencies.

Here are items to be certain to include in your primary first aid kit:

- Nitrile gloves
- Blister care products
- Band-aids - multiple sizes and waterproof type
- Ace wrap and athletic tape
- Alcohol wipes and antibiotic ointment
- Irrigation syringe
- Tweezers, nail clippers, trauma shears, safety pins
- Small Ziplock bags containing contaminated trash

It is recommended to also keep a secondary first aid kit, especially when hiking, for more serious injuries or medical emergencies. Items in this should include:

- Blood clotting sponges
- Sterile gauze pads
- Trauma pads
- Second-skin/burn treatment
- Triangular bandages/sling

- Butterfly strips
- Tincture of benzoin
- Medications (ibuprofen, acetaminophen, antihistamine, aspirin, etc.)
- Thermometer
- CPR mask
- Wilderness medicine handbook
- Antivenin

There is so much more to explore, but this is a great start.

For information on all national parks, visit: www.nps.gov.

This site will give you information on up-to-date entrance fees and how to purchase a park pass for unlimited access to national and state parks. This site will also introduce you to all of the trails of each park.

Always check before you travel to destinations to make sure there are no closures. Some hikes close when there is heavy rain or snow in the area, and other parks close parts of their land for the migration of wildlife. Attractions may change their hours or temporarily shut down for various reasons. Check the websites for the most up-to-date information.

Made in United States
Orlando, FL
18 November 2024

54062313R00075